THE ANCIENT CODE
A SERPENT FIRE

The Ancient Code - A Serpent Fire
By Michael Feeley

Published 2018 by Sazmick Books
Web: www.sazmickbooks.com
Web: www.michael-feeley.com

Book and Cover Design - Sarah Feeley, Sazmick Books

© Copyright 2018 Michael Feeley. All rights reserved.
No part of this book may be reproduced, stored in a retrieval system, or transmitted by any means without the written permission of the author.
Please note: The views in this book are not necessarily those of the publisher.

British Library Cataloguing-in Publication Data.
A catalogue record for this book is available from the British Library.

ISBN: 978-1-912400-13-3 (Paperback)
ISBN: 978-1-912400-14-0 (Ebook)

Printed and bound in the UK
using sustainable resources

THE ANCIENT CODE
A SERPENT FIRE

MICHAEL FEELEY

CONTENTS

Acknowledgements v
Foreword (By Meria Heller) ix
About The Author xiii
About The Book xvii

Chapter 1: The One Time Beginning: The Creation Of The Universe ... 1
Chapter 2: The History Of Hu-Man 9
Chapter 3: My Weird Paranormal Life 17
Chapter 4: The Ego Of Man: When Knowledge Became Concealed .. 33
Chapter 5: The Third Dimensional Prison: Life Without Parole 53
Chapter 6: The Bible Code: What The Priesthoods Don't Want You To Know 67
Chapter 7: Adam & Eve And The Garden Of Eden: The Inner Body 73
Chapter 8: Moses: The Mozilla Firefox 79
Chapter 9: Noah: Let Us Now Flood The World With Some Truth 93
Chapter 10: Mary And Joseph: The Water And The Seed 99
Chapter 11: Jesus: What Is The Truth For Christ Sake? 107
Chapter 12: The Ascended Christ: Post Crucifixion - Back In The Heavens 123
Chapter 13: Hwt-Ka-Ptah: The Pyramid Code – The Mystery Solved ... 135
Chapter 14: Stonehenge: The Cyclopean Ritual 179
Chapter 15: King Arthur: The Great Bear 197
Chapter 16: Santa Claus: The Holy Colostrum 203
Chapter 17: Pirates: The Inner Treasure 209
Chapter 18: Above Government: Crop Secret 215
Chapter 19: The Path Of Transcendence 219
Chapter 20: Conclusion 229

FOREWORD

By Meria Heller, Author, Teacher and host/producer of the 18 years and continuing podcast "The Meria Heller Show" at www.Meria.net

I've had the pleasure of interviewing Michael Feeley on my international podcast. His work is excellent and it was easy for me to resonate with it. As listeners of my work know I continuously say "the only ticket out of here is a spiritual one". Michael's book explains the who and how's in his book.

Imagine that you are living in a false reality, a hologram of sorts, a computer game. Add to that everything you've ever been taught has been a lie. You are merely an avatar in a computer game being moved around by what I like to call your over soul. Waking up from the "dream state" can be very painful and hard to adjust to. Similar to the red pill, blue pill choices shown in the movie "The Matrix". But another saying I have is "I'd rather know than not know".

I had an NDE (near death experience) when I was four years old. It was back in Brooklyn, New York in the 1950's. When I awoke I knew things. Things no four year old should know. The illusion, time travel, parallel lives, different dimensions and more. Wasn't easy being a kid with all that knowledge in a predominantly Italian/Catholic neighbourhood. My messages were not well received.

Today it is many years later and the things I saw and warned people about have become "reality". My "gift" of sight has helped me with my dissecting what is called the "news" here for my show and audience. Of course my work draws a lot of interest and authors who are on a spiritual path to en-lighten-ment. One of those authors is Michael Feeley. His story and evolvement is interesting enough, but his work goes beyond that into exposing the true reality here.

If you can wrap your mind around the fact that we have been controlled and divided for ages by the two main systems of control: religion and politics, you will be able to delve into this work and truly understand what it's all about.

I was raised in religion for years and the only thing that made sense to me was one line in the bible – "God is love". All else is hogwash. Love is what it's all about and the strongest force in the universe. Michael explains the falsehoods we've been taught by religion very well in his books. What is god? Read on and learn.

Everything here is sound and vibration. Thoughts do have wings. This planet is ruled by secret societies and evil bloodlines that serve unseen masters. That may sound crazy until you start doing the homework. Their goal is trans-humanism and total control of our consciousness and world. Without a true understanding of the codes, cover ups and secrets put in place a long time ago – you will continue to play their computer game and never be able to progress your way out of it. I've spent the better part of my life investigating all that is. The truth is out there for those willing to do the research and resonate with truth.

We live in dastardly times for the human race: threat of nuclear war more imminent than ever, poisons and technology in our air, water and food. All around the corner to take not only our jobs, but our souls as well – makes it all the more urgent to do the homework, support those brave enough to stand up and tell you the truth. I suggest starting with all of Michael's books. I have many spiritual shows with solutions on my site as well to help in your journey.

Recognize the "angels" that walk among us to awaken us to who and what we really are. As my teacher Sun Bear used to say "If you knew what walked alongside you every minute of every day you'd fear nothing".

I'm proud to be able to work with Michael, and I'm sure you will resonate to his work!

Meria Heller
www.Meria.net

ABOUT THE AUTHOR

Michael was born in 1972 in the West Midlands region of the UK. He completed a standard secondary education at school attaining several 'O' level, ordinary level, qualifications.

From a very young age Michael knew he felt different and regularly questioned Earthly existence in often quiet contemplation, although he doesn't recall any strange activity or visitations during his childhood.

He was comfortable and happy in his solitude within the fortress that acted as his bedroom, listening to music in the days before computers. Michael knew that hidden in architecture and Church windows and brand names and logos and celebrity and political public hand gestures there was a secret language being spoken beyond the scope of the ordinary man and women.

Michael Feeley is the real life Robert Langdon, the character played by Tom Hanks in the movie 'The Da Vinci Code'. He has deciphered many ancient codes that have remained hidden for Thousands of years.

He has identified the true identity of Jesus Christ and Mary Magdalene and many of the most famous biblical characters! He has uncovered the true purpose of the likes of Stonehenge and the Pyramids of Egypt and has solved many of the other great mysteries of our time. He has joined the dots that have been missed by many prominent others and has linked ancient civilizations together, whom we are told never had any communications with one another, through a 'Unique Blueprint' that he has discovered!

Michael learned in later life that he was a descendent of ancient Irish Celtic Kings, who were themselves related to Pharaonic Egypt.

He joined the Police force in 1992 and was a front-line officer in England's two biggest and major cities and was regarded as an expert witness in court. He was an investigator of all levels of crime and a crime scene forensic preserver and evidential writer. He received many accolades and awards and recognition for his work, including official commendations for bravery. But in 2009 that was all about to change and in the years following 2009 paranormal activity was a daily occurrence in his life and Michael now is and continues to be a multiple paranormal and UFO experiencer and has also seen and experienced multidimensional reality. Michael left his career in the police force in 2009 as a result of constant paranormal activity and other reasons more personal, going against the tide as the world approached a global recession, leaving secure employment as many were losing their jobs.

He now uses his 17 years of investigative training and evidence gathering experience to decipher many hidden codes concealed within the ancient monuments and even the most read book in the world, the Bible. Michael recognises what is known as a Modus Operandi meaning "method of operation" in Latin, in other words a method used by groups or individuals to complete a task, using the same technique repeatedly to achieve their aims. The task in this case is to deceive the population and to prevent sacred information from reaching that population, by the creation of a smoke-screen of false icons and stores and inaccurate mainstream information. And it has worked very well for them.

Michael was given a Spiritual Gnostic Golden key in 2009, meaning the right to know this sacred knowledge, which was seen as a privilege and only for certain eyes and ears of the chosen. He now passes that knowledge onto many others through numerous global radio interviews, including 'Unknown Country' with Whitley Strieber, talks, large conferences and TV appearances. Michael, even to this day, continues to see the number 22 which again is the Gnostic number of divine knowledge, the word Gnostic itself means to know or knowledge of the divine/divine knowledge. 22 is also significant in Hebrew and Egyptian principles as both of their alphabets have 22 letters and the Gnostics concealed God (Aleph) within the alphabet and also Christ, QRST, which becomes more relevant later in the book.

It is the Gnostic principle that 'only the eyes that can see and ears that can hear' will come into this knowledge and when we look at the bible it is telling us this in an esoteric way, as per usual, with the statement *"All eyes shall see him"*. The eye referred to is the third eye (pineal gland) the spiritual eye, (and internal genetics that I will go into later in the Jesus chapter) and when we see Christ on his way to the Crucifixion the cross was being carried by a character called Simon which derives from the Hebrew Shi'mon which means 'to listen'. The pineal gland (single eye) also responds to other stimuli like sound, hence to hear is relevant to this too.

In ancient times the four elements were namely Fire, Water, Air and Earth but today these are Carbon, Oxygen, Nitrogen and Hydrogen, which in element numbers collectively equal 22. Certain ancient cultures believed that God was the four elements and spoke to them through the four elements, given the name Yod-He-Wau-He which in tetragrammaton, the divine name in four letters, is YHWH, later to become Yahweh or the Latin equivalent JHVH which is Jehovah. In other words the number 22 represents a divine or higher connection.

In a life that was once 'normal' for him normal can never be a part of his life again! Michael has also seen a Red Rose manifesting out of his bedroom ceiling and the Red Rose is symbolic of impending spiritual knowledge.

Michael has been intentionally given secret information in order to share it far and wide to help humanity. There is a code, a secret language being spoken, so secret that it is hidden within the architecture of buildings, company logos and brand names, words and letters, belief systems and religions and their allegorical icons and figures of worship. This code spans across the ancient world and joins hands with the modern world, surviving time and surviving the awareness and the attention of the general population for hundreds and thousands of years.

Join Michael as he reveals the many secrets that have baffled humanities greatest minds and uncovers the deep and interwoven web of secret and deciphered codes... 'The Ancient Code' is about to be revealed for the first time outside of the sacred and secret walls of the mystery schools, a code that the priesthoods do not want you to know!

They are about to become very disappointed as the fabric of their secrecy becomes unwoven, stitch by stitch and the prison gates that surround the human mind unlocks and the prison walls come falling down...

ABOUT THE BOOK

The world is full of great mysteries, the unsolved, the guessed at and then we have some, or least a few of the answers.

For many thousands of years there has been an undercurrent of secrecy around knowledge and information that could lead to the advancement of humanity as a race of beings. With this knowledge we could reconnect with the cosmos, from which we have become a segregated species.

There is a secret code that spans throughout the ancient gnostic world that is hidden from all but the selected few. This code, regardless of the civilization encoding it, speaks of the same message!

In this book the author takes you back in time to the original creation of everything, to man's arrival on the scene, through to where knowledge was shared. And it then takes you through our downfall as this knowledge became separated from general circulation and deliberately hidden from our view by a select few sects and brotherhoods who wanted to keep it to themselves for themselves creating a series of false stories to substitute truth so that we can never be as enlightened as them. The same group have forged our reality to one which they wish for us to see, it is not real and it doesn't have to be this way.

Religion is the most divisive of these man-made creations, keeping the people of the world at odds by taking our focus outside of ourselves as we constantly wait for our heavenly saviours to pass the responsibility onto for our actions.

What the author has achieved with this book, after many years of deep guided research, is to decipher the spoken languages of the initiates and reveal the true meanings of the great mysteries of our time. Such as the true deeper scriptures and meanings of the Bible and its famous characters, concealed by a Bible code, the real purpose for the Pyramids of Egypt and Stonehenge and Norse and Greek mythology and even King

Arthur and Santa Claus, all of which are connected, as you will see by the conclusion of this book. The author even shows you a connection between the monuments of planet Earth and those on planet Mars!

Michael's new book *The Ancient Code - A Serpent Fire*, not only exposes thousands of years of biblical and ecclesiastical secrecy but it also joins the dots of the advanced knowledge of the ancients, deliberately concealed from us by the priesthoods and it path finds a way of transition beyond our third dimensional prison!

So prepare for the revealing of a secret and complex world of coded messages and languages used by the chosen initiates who hold the key that unlocks the door of knowledge as Michael goes deeper than ever before into the world of hidden knowledge and encoded secrecy, Join Michael as he awakens the Serpent Fire within you through the coded gifts left for us by the advanced pathfinders of the human race...

1

The One Time Beginning: The Creation Of The Universe

Perfection realises that it is empty space without any experience. Dark light is widely prevalent and there is not yet any electromagnetic energy to create the frequency that will become visible light. It has always been, always was and always will be, the concept of which is both mind blowing and inconceivable to the human mind. It is, in its current state, self-awareness as the unfulfilled whole.

A pure supreme mathematical mind has a thought, an abstract concept that it must create reality in an instant, it must create the self-ability to live and experience, to expand out and then return from a singularity that constantly repeats itself in a cycle of microcosm-macrocosm until the return to singularity once again having now sensed and lived all eventuality and every possibility through extensions of itself. It is to become Mathematics that connects the physical and metaphysical worlds. A singularity where all parallels cross and dense matter and the time-space continuum become infinite and once again irrelevant.

The biblical father's house of many rooms, the house is the mind of many different fields and planes of mental activity. All that exists is an abstract concept of pure mathematics, encoded number sequences, finite and infinite fractals that will later form shapes and instructions to give us the building blocks of life. Then all at once a 'One Time Beginning' a Eureka moment, a flash of energy and light, the Big bang and then the universe houses life as we know it, scientifically proven by the 'Cosmic Background Explorer (COBE) experiment of 1989-1993.

The many souls are created in the womb of the sky. Our universe becomes part of the multiverse and so on. The human soul was to be later recorded in 1907 by Dr McDougall and measured to be ¾ ounce or 21 grams. Sub-atomic particles travel back and forwards in time, Quantum Tunnelling, time being the duration of existence, which will become pinnacle in our third dimensional reality. Electromagnetic dualistic opposing energy, now married together by a neutral force, created visible light, light itself then slowing down its oscillations to create dense matter resulting in what we know and understand to be physicality.

The same electromagnetic forces create colour by their different vibrations and oscillations. The electromagnetic light that arches becomes the angels and archangels (angles and arch-angles) of light with helical waves as wings.

In the universe there are two forms of light, the visible light and the invisible light known as dark matter. It is still light, black light, but we cannot see it, our eyes simply cannot pick up its frequency, but nevertheless it exists and it is there. In science the photon, which is a particle of light, is known as a 'Messenger Particle' and angel means messenger. The photon constantly travels at the speed of light and is therefore external to time, it is outside of our time-space continuum and we know from the 'Double Slit' experiment that photons are conscious, they have awareness and are aware of themselves and aware of being watched when they are being observed! The photon is the Quantum of the 'Electromagnetic field' and the electromagnetic field is a dual charge of electricity and magnetism, positive and negative charge combined! Colour is simply a frequency within the electromagnetic field and the human Soul is made of photonic light. The forces of the gaseous Ether are at work creating a turbulent environment of sonoluminescent storms where sound causes electrical lightning strikes. The collision of atoms and particles create sound which in turn creates the light.

Black light and dark matter becomes cosmic glue holding all together. The stars and planets are introduced to mathematical sound, the nodes of standing waves, that sends them on a pre-ordained and pre-destined space journey, all programmed to stop a certain distance apart from each other to maintain relativity and locking them into a gravitational pull and orbit, a whirlwind of endless rotation. The stars themselves are made of plasma which is a distinctive stage of matter. Stars give off star frequencies some of them having human consciousness raising properties. Earth's poles push together causing the Dynamo effect of convection within Earth's molten core, creating a protective shield around the globe.

Particles and Sub-atomic particles act as vehicles on the interstellar highway dashing around, with electrons orbiting the nucleus of the atom in the exact same replicated way that the planets of Earth's solar system orbit the sun. The nucleus is the centre of the atom and the Sun is the centre of the Solar system, and all are displaying the divine geometric shape, the sphere or circle. All locked into each other's orbit, the exact correct distance apart to do so, causing relativity. Energy is the universal powerhouse and energy is the product of mass + light squared (E=MC2). E = mc2 is an equation derived by the future Earthly twentieth-century physicist Albert Einstein, in which E represents units of energy, M represents units of mass, and C2 is the speed of light squared, or multiplied by itself. Because the speed of light is a very large number and is multiplied by itself, this equation points out how a small amount of matter can release a huge amount of energy, as in a nuclear reaction. The physical finite world is governed by finite fractals and the infinite universe is governed by infinite fractals (Duplication). One of the most remarkable mathematical codes is the Mandelbrot set, a complex series of numbers that will not deviate and can only be replicated by computer, a complex series that is self-replicating according to some predetermined rule. Creating a finite mathematical equation of ZN, the set of complex numbers C for which the iteration Zn+1 = zn2 + C produces finite ZN for all N when started at Z0 = 0 duplicating forever in the nonphysical world.

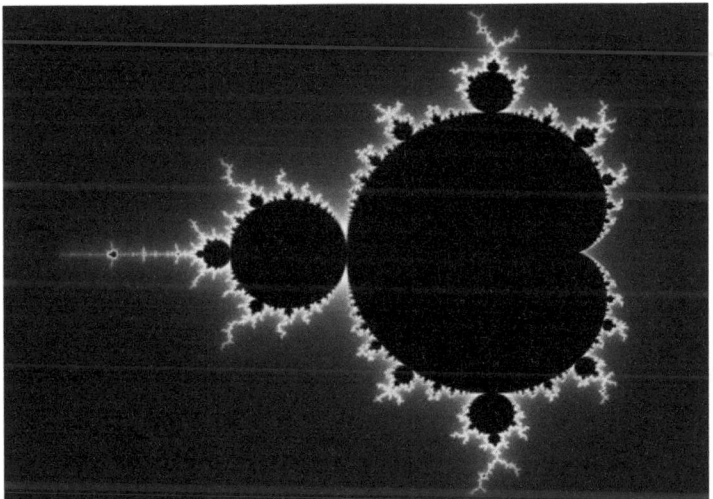

(Mandelbrot Set)

Centripetal and centrifugal forces, of the gravity family, act as an opposing gravitational force, In Newtonian mechanics, the centrifugal force is an inertial force directed away from the axis of rotation that appears to act on all objects when viewed in a rotating frame of reference and Centripetal force is a force that makes a body follow a curved path. Its direction is always orthogonal to the motion of the body and towards the fixed point of the instantaneous centre of curvature of the path. Isaac Newton described it as a force by which bodies are drawn or impelled or in any way tends, towards a point as to a centre. In Newtonian mechanics, gravity provides the centripetal force responsible for astronomical orbits. Nature's anomalies adhere to the 19.5 degree effect on all spinning bodies of the solar system, North or South latitude of the equator. An equator is the intersection of the surface of a rotating spheroid with the plane perpendicular to the axis of rotation and midway between its poles. On Earth, the Equator is an imaginary line on the surface, equidistant from the North and South Poles, dividing the Earth into Northern and Southern Hemispheres. It is about 40,075 kilometres long, of which 78.7% lies across water and 21.3% over land. Gravitropism is introduced encoding plants and flowers to grow both downwards from their roots and simultaneously upwards against gravity.

Everything is given a mathematical programmed code that it will strictly adhere to, a code that will form its dimensions and diameters throughout the existence of its species and kind. Mathematics that would also later be used as coordinates in Earth's future but now her ancient past to locate the worlds famous monuments and beyond like a giant encoded mathematical satellite navigation system.

Nature is given the Fibonacci sequence of stability and guidance and the universe, one verse, is an endless dance of sound, light and geometry, geometry of divinity, GOD! All of which contain a mathematical code.

Dimensions are formed, a dimension being the minimum amount of coordinates required to specify a point within, providing rooms within the dodecahedron system and wavelengths separate lifeforms behind a small veil of frequency spectra so that they remain unseen but for a brief glimpse as they tune into one another. Seen with microscopic eye, floating numbers whizz passed at speed, I have actually looked up at the clouds and have seen numbers (1's & 2's) in the shape and position of a cloud where a cloud was first situated for it then to morph back into a cloud, the numbers then disappearing. The solar system and Zodiac are formed, the celestial narrative, the wheel of Gad or as it would be later religiously and biblically translated, the will of God.

Then Humanity as we know it becomes a manifested universal presence and given an Inner Consciousness, a mind, a brain to function and to be aware of self, through the various stages of advancement and development, in-built with the potential to connect the Inner consciousness to outer consciousness (higher consciousness) and therefore re-connect to the God-Mind, the brain being a smaller version of the god mind with the power of thought and manifestation of that thought. The thinking man is connected to this universal creative mind by the power of thought. We become a manifestation of the 'Adam Kadmon', which is the first manifestation of abstract space, the idea before the physical. Man is locked into chronobiology, the night and day cycles of earth.

Discoveries come by intuition from a higher plane of consciousness when the mind in open to new ideas or knowledge. Not just on Earth but spread out all across the universe in different locations and planetary systems. Mathematical PI omitting a frequency of 432 Hertz is used to balance the third dimension and will later be in used within the Great Pyramid of Egypt. However for now humanity is locked into a narrow bandwidth of 7 colours and 5 senses and it sees less than 1% of the available frequency spectra. We are locked into a concept called time, a duration of existence, a component quantity of various measurements used to sequence events, to compare the duration of events or the intervals between them, and to quantify rates of change of quantities in material reality or in the conscious experience. Time is often referred to as a fourth dimension, along with three spatial dimensions.

As a third dimensional creation we skip from one block of third dimensional time to another which in order to continue to function as dimensionality must have a definitive separation which is our life and death cycle, the transition from linear to lateral time, a change of viewpoint as the movie slides that are our life flicker from one scene to the next.

The micro-macro effect trickles down from the gigantic spirals of nebulas and galaxies to the smallest of creatures on Earth to the smallest known existence in the universe, the sub-atomic world that is both inside and outside of us, which in itself is a bottle sized universe, an organic atom. Everything has a place and everything is a part of everything else. There is no separation, even in what we consider to be empty space it is really full, there is only a loss of sight through a frequency filter, not emptiness or separation.

The whole universe is made with panpsychism where everything has a consciousness.

Once we know this we can once again begin to think big!

"If you want to find the secrets of the universe, think in terms of energy, frequency and vibration" – Nikola Tesla

WE ARE...

2

The History Of Hu-Man

A biological eco system of life has now been created and that life fills the universe, it is new and it is vibrant. The micro unseen world upon Earth lives seemingly separate from the rest of creation but it is well and truly connected by slender threads that are unbreakably strong.

If you are to believe Darwinism primates were to become man, but if that was the case and we had developed from them then there would be no primates on planet Earth today but there is and I do not subscribe to Darwin's theory of evolution. Homo-erectus (upright man), the earliest known humans, entered the scene around 1.9 million years ago existing from the end of the Pliocene to the later Pleistocene epoch, if fossil evidence is correct, and is believed to have originated in Africa.

If we use Qatam physics or as it is known Melanin Physics this branch of science proves this theory to be correct and proves that the black races were the original inhabitants of Earth. Homo-erectus spread across the globe from this point of African origin. Melanin is simply the vibration of light giving us a certain skin colour. It is a dark brown to black pigment occurring in the hair, skin, and iris of the eye in people and animals. It is responsible for tanning of skin exposed to sunlight.

They sometimes used caves as shelters but they often built shelters out of tree branches, with their chopping tools they hacked branches from young trees, probably trimming off the twigs, and then they poked the branches into the ground in rough circle, holding them in place by piling rocks against them. The tops of the branches were probably bent and twisted together so that the finished hut was more or less tent shaped. The remains of such a hut has been found holes made by branches that were pushed into the ground, rocks that were once piled against these branches, and a circle of stones in the centre where a fire was kept burning. But although these people could build crude huts, they did not live together in villages. They would eat meat and berries, fish and eggs. There is evidence that Homo-erectus could speak, but not to the extent of modern humans which is relevant and connected as the word HU, as in human, in Egyptian circles is the power of utterance and the spoken word. Homo-erectus lived up until possibly around 35,000 years ago which in science is a pinnacle time of Human evolution.

It is around this time that humanity advanced at a rapid rate. Then there is a big gap in the theory of evolution where Homo-erectus became Homo-Sapien, meaning intelligent man. This happened far too fast for the process of ordinary evolution and it was now that man became able to comprehend complex things and speak complex languages. Something had happened to advance the then human race quite revolutionary.

There is a theory that picks up this enigma, which is of extra-terrestrial intervention from a race of beings known as the Annunaki, which means 'Those who from Heaven to Earth came' who were evidently far more advanced than Earth humans, simply because they had been around longer than we had. It is claimed that they tinkered with human genetics mixing primate genes with that of existing humans creating what we are today, Homo-Sapien. This story was made world famous by the late author Zecharia Sitchen who gave the world his translations of the Sumerian Scrolls (Sumer being modern day Iraq) which championed this version of history. Central to the story were characters by the name of Enki and Enlil who were the Gods of land and sky, the snake brothers (Sheti). Their Father and leader was Anu and they were allegedly conveyed in a planet sized space craft known as planet X or Nibiru which has a 3600 year Earth cycle. Sitchen claimed that these scrolls stated that this Alien race came to Earth to mine for Gold to aid the dwindling atmosphere of their own planet and used the new humans they had created as a slave workforce to do the hard labour on their behalf.

I am a multiple paranormal and UFO experiencer, I know that what we deem as aliens exist, I have seen them. They have been here throughout our history and are still here in differing capacities. However, although I agree in principle with the idea of an intervention of some kind, I have a different interpretation of the Sumerian scrolls based on an ancient blueprint that I have discovered that actually connects these ancient cultures in a way that has not been admitted to or publically acknowledged by the mainstream historians. One word that is constant throughout this book is 'Consciousness' and with each of the chapters presented you will notice that all are really referring to this fact, it is indeed the 'Ancient Code'. However I do acknowledge that humanity has been genetically interfered with.

So with that in mind here's my interpretation of what the Sumerian scrolls are really saying and telling us and it is genetic. The bible talks about the first man and woman being Adam and Eve, which I will go into more detail about in later chapters, but that too is really a genetic story.

So now for the scrolls...

In my opinion Zecharia Sitchen has made a literal face value translation and has missed the deeper message which I have found to be that of genetics and enlightened consciousness spanning all across and connecting the people of the ancient world. The Annunaki story has Anu as the chief Sumerian God and Anu means the 'ultimate physical atom of creation' and the word Nakki means to change...therefore the atom has been changed which I acknowledge does support the Sitchen translations. Enki and Enlil, the snake brothers, are the two strands of the double helix of human DNA, which resembles two snakes coiled together. Many people are seeing what appears to be an object adjacent to the solar Sun and claim this to be the planet X, Nibiru, spoken about in the Sitchen translations, the home of the Annunaki. Nibiru however means 'Wandering planet' and in Egyptian astronomy their name for the planet Venus is Neb-Heru, (house of Horus) which is far too close to be a coincidence. Venus's orbit wonders noticeably and is therefore known as the 'Wandering planet'. Venus is also pinnacle in the raising of consciousness vibrating at 442 hertz. Nibiru is supposedly a spaceship for these alien beings but it only has the power of orbit rather than trajectory, in which case how did it get to where it is now meant to be? It could not have been flown as a craft with only orbiting power.

(Sumerian Scrolls/God Enlil)

When we see the carvings of the Annunaki Gods they are usually presented to us like this picture. The component parts of the carvings are again telling us about consciousness. The Pine-Cone being held is the Pineal Gland which is a part of the human endocrine system known as the third eye and can also be seen as a statue at various significant locations such as the Vatican in Rome, Vatican derives from Vatika which means third eye (Pineal Gland). The Gods are usually carrying a bag which no one has ever been able to decipher. This is symbolic of hidden secret knowledge destined for the chosen and worthy initiates.

Within the brain there is a part called the Cerebellum meaning little brain and it deals with equilibrium and when we reach the Egyptian chapter the importance of balance will become apparent. In the Annunaki carvings the Cerebellum is represented by the two wings which are the two lateral hemispheres of the Cerebellum itself. They are separated by a region known as 'Vermis' which in Latin means serpent. The whole picture is telling us of the endocrine system of the human brain. Endocrine mean 'Secretion within' and secretion gives rise to secret. Our own consciousness is a big secret hidden from us all.

The aspect of the story where the Annunaki mined for Gold is really again talking about searching for enlightenment, gold being the colour associated with knowledge and consciousness itself. Another aspect of the Annunaki story tells us that they brought the Moon with them when they arrived at planet Earth, it also states that when they arrived they found life already here!

Scientifically this cannot be correct for the following reasons. The Moon has the same Isotopes which are chemical elements as the Earth and is the same age, therefore it was created in the same region of sky at the same time. The Moon is a planetary stabilizer for Earth keeping her at a 23.5 degree tilt and without it there cannot be life on Earth, therefore if the Annunaki brought the Moon here with them they could not have discovered life here on Earth when they arrived. This 23.5 degree tilt enables Earth's oceans and waters to remain a liquid, gives us the four seasons and keeps the planet at an inhabitable temperature that sustains life.

If you divide the circumference of the sun by that of the Moon and multiply by 100 you get the polar circumference of Earth. The Moon is exactly 400 times smaller than the Sun and exactly 400 times closer to Earth than the Sun giving the illusion that they are the same size, this gives us the eclipses we see in our skies at various times. The Moon also revolves exactly one hundredth of the speed that the Earth turns on its axis. Therefore it is original purposeful locating.

The Moon, as a side note, is pinnacle to the female body which is locked into its cycles which I will go into a little later.

I am not denying genetic tinkering, it is the most likely cause of our sudden advancement, but as I use that word Consciousness again I am saying that as with the whole coded theme of this book there is a world of sacred knowledge that is being deliberately concealed from us and clues to this sacred knowledge are cleverly hidden in plain sight within such works as the scrolls and many other significant places.

But all we need do is look beyond the upper surfaces and literal translations of historical content and we will see the true meanings.

3

My Weird Paranormal Life

In this chapter I will be detailing some of my own experiences that prove, at least prove to me, that there is something beyond this world and realm, I know because I have seen it too many times and in the following chapter I will be detailing some of the groups that try at all costs to hide this fact and why and how they are doing it.

As stated in the about the author section I grew up in the industrial heart of England in the West Midlands, the only child of a working father and a full time mother. There was nothing particularly strange or unusual about my upbringing other than the fact that I knew something was different about me and I used to silently question the world in general which made very little sense from a logical prospective. I was not into large social groups of friends just the few close and entrusted ones whom I felt comfortable with. I was not into macho fighting and repelled any such activity around me, sticking up for the victim of these actions whenever I saw it and befriending the children at school who no one seemed to want to associate with. I did not care about what people thought of this Good Samaritan conquest, I did what I felt was right regardless of the opinion of others.

Like most other children I attended nursery, junior school and then finally secondary school as part of my standard state education. At about the age of 15 or 16 I had an overwhelming urge to be a police officer and everything from that point on was geared towards my chosen career, all jobs that I took were only ever going to be temporary position until I achieved my goal which took many years and lots of determination.

But I eventually succeeded and in 1992 I become a police officer. 18 weeks of residential training on a pass or fail course, weekly examinations with a 70% pass mark, morning uniform inspections and constant ongoing assessments of paperwork skills and scenario based tests.

On the day itself I woke up with an excited anticipation but yet it was masked with a dull sadness as I was to leave my family home and town of origin for the first time in my life. If I had my own two feet now was the time I needed to stand on them. I said my goodbyes and boarded the train for the journey into a new life, forever aware that the old life was attempting to magnetically cling onto me, but my new life was one that I had dreamed of for a long time and it was strong enough to out run any gravitational force pulling me back. Would it live up to my expectations or would it fail miserably, have I made a mistake or was it a good choice? Only time would tell, but I had at least made a choice.

I arrived at my destination, the training college and was allocated into a class and I met up with my tutors and classmates who would be an extension of me for the next 18 weeks of gruelling exams, morning uniform inspections, tested scenarios and continuous tests to assess our general ability for the role. A high failure rate was the norm, in fact a 35% failure rate, but I was determined not to be that statistic. A doctor and several nurses were permanently on-site for the stress factor and general push and pull on the body as the weeks took their toll. With each week the horizon drew closer, that light at the end of the tunnel came forever nearer to the passing out parade that would see us leave here and venture onto the mean streets to start our new careers. 18 exams later, 18 weeks of shouting and screaming at the hands of the ex-army drill instructors and 18 weeks of torrential tests had now come to a delightful end. The day had now arrived just as fast as our family had arrived to witness their loved ones parade for the last time on this famous and hallowed training ground. Tears flooded the parade square and army band music set the rhythm, our battle lines were drawn as we stood to attention before the final march and inspection. A rigorous regime likened to the military by those who had left it and escaped it to come here. The sound of marching feet took centre stage as the formation gathered in synchronicity like the crashing of the ocean's waves upon rocks of the shoreline.

Memories formed and life time associates made, we all wished each other well as we left the training centre which had been our home for over 4 months for the last time. The child had become the adult and the apprentice had become the fully fledged. But the day finally arrived and it was my passing out parade, a spectacle for family who had made the long journey to the police training college, a journey I had made weekly.

It was Christmas and I went home for 2 weeks leave going back to my old life for a short time but I was a different person, I now had my career and my dream had been fulfilled. Now all that was left was 2 years' worth of probation.

If I had had retrospect in a bottle then things may have been different from the onset, I may never have joined had I have known that I would be leaving in 2009. I had never anticipated leaving, I was going to be there forever and a day and then some more, the police was my first marriage and those who get married don't often contemplate divorce, it can just happen. Sometimes life has different plans, life directs you to where you need to be at that time often for a greater purpose than we can possibly know at the time. Sometimes we find ourselves unknowingly stepping from each stepping stone venturing in a direction we cannot immediately see. The lesson that it taught me and the experience that it gave me has now come into fruition with my new path.

My police career was on the front-line dealing with emergency calls, victims of crime, arresting and processing offenders and later securing convictions at court. I also dealt with and investigated all levels of crime. I was a well decorated officer with many awards to my name including bravery awards. It was during my time as a police officer that I met my wife Sarah and our relationship blossomed during inner city riots and many long hours within police vehicles spanning from early morning to early morning without a gap in between.

Both Sarah and I began to feel very disillusioned from about midway through 2007 onwards, starting initially as minor gripes but later turning to actions close to rebellion for a system that was no longer compatible with our moral standards. But the pinnacle year for us both and for me was 2009 when we actually resigned from the police force into the unknown with nothing to actually go to. That year was to change our lives and my life forever in more ways than one as I was introduced to the Paranormal and other worlds and existences. Here's how it began!

My wife Sarah had once been told that she had the spirit of a young girl with her, as a child she lived in the area that this spirit girl had lived, on the same region of land. Sarah's family was aware of the story of this girl and the rumour was that she had died of Weil's disease.

Through the help of a psychic medium this version of events was far from correct. When I came onto the scene I also inherited this spirit and around the 2008/2009 time we both visited the same medium who gave us both an individual reading. From that reading it was established that this spirit girl, named Sarah Jenson, wanted us to investigate her death, as she was "taken by another's hands" which we took to mean she was murdered which actually turned out to be correct. Sarah and I attended the central Birmingham library (UK), which was the area in question to search for any registered deaths in that name, but the problem we faced was that we didn't have any actual time frame to work off. We had little or no clue as to the time-frame when this event actually took place.

So we decided to pick a date at random and went back to the 1960's, and a little earlier not for any particular reason other than we just had to choose a start point. We couldn't find anything relevant having spent the complete day at the library looking through hours and hours of slides of registered deaths. We then decided, albeit a little frustrating, that we would have to stop and give up on our search for answers, a discussion we had privately over lunch, or at least that's what we thought, but it was overheard by Sarah Jenson as we were to later find out. That decision was to be a negative turning point for us! Things now started to take a nose dive and we would have double glazed windows at home smashed in front of our eyes from the inside, with no sign of anyone or anything that may have been responsible. I spoke to the medium on the phone and explained that we needed help, but as I was talking to her our house became calm again. The medium stated that Sarah Jenson was now with her and that she was upset with us stating that we didn't help her as we said we would. We arranged to collect the medium the next day from her own house so that she could resolve the matter or at least help in some way. That night was about to become the scene from a horror movie, involving my wife and I as the cast.

It was now the February of 2009 (February 8th) and whilst I was sitting at home on the laptop computer I could feel something entering my body and attempting to take control of it and possess it. I became very snappy and instantly angry which was not my personality coming through, it was the entity who was trying to possess me. I managed to resist and the sensation disappeared. Within a short time we could smell flowers in the room and the radiator which was on hot suddenly drained of any heat and went freezing cold, this was not a mechanical issue.

We had to leave the house and stay at Sarah's mother's home for the evening such were the events taking place. We arrived and spent the night there going to bed around 1.30am in the early hours of 9th February in a bedroom which was a ground floor garage conversion. The time was now about 3.30am and I suddenly remember being taken back to an old wooden type room that had a bed, which I was laying in, a window opposite and a wooden door in the right hand corner of the room. I remember the door suddenly creaking open the wind of which caused the light blue coloured curtains to move and it was at that point I heard the voice of a young girl saying "He's here" I cannot remember much from that point on, and I didn't recognise the girl's voice. However Sarah told me that I was screaming hysterically in utter fright and that she couldn't calm me down. It was like I was being attacked and it later turned out that I actually was being attacked. As I came around I felt tingly but back in my room. In another twist of fate as I looked over to Sarah she was the one screaming hysterically and not me, but when she came round she couldn't remember herself screaming. The same thing was happening to the both of us at the same time, each another's audience without us realising that it was happening to us personally or individually, just the other person almost like an individual yet joint multi-dimensional slip. Sarah and I got out of bed and sat downstairs eager for daylight to arrive, terrified and baffled.

Later that morning we boarded our vehicle to collect the medium but as we were doing so she called saying she couldn't make it. Needless to say she was convinced otherwise and we continued to her house to collect her and as we arrived she was nervously standing outside her front door. She told us that during the morning her coffee cup had been moved from the kitchen to her living room window sill and had had a spoon placed inside it. She also said that her washing machine that was not switched on had lifted off the floor by itself and although she'd been a medium for a long time dealing with all aspects of the 'Other Side' this had been the first time she'd been scared and had had to leave her own house.

We made the hour or so journey to my house and it was now through the medium that we actually found out what had happened.

Sarah Jenson had been abused and murdered by her stepfather who smothered her in the year 1850, Victorian England, hence why we were not able to locate any trace during our library visit, we simply had not gone back far enough in time. At this point we discovered that his spirit was also with us and that he'd been causing much of the problems we were facing leading up to the 9th February event! He gave us him name as John Berkshire. The medium stated that this day was the anniversary of the murder hence why we smelled flowers the night before and that we had actually relived this girl's last moments alive, which is what my wife and I both witnessed in each other screaming!

She stated that Sarah Jenson would sit crouched up in the left hand corner of our bedroom below the window for considerable time frames, I didn't know if that meant our time or hers. This rang true because leading up to the event we used to have a stray cat who would occasionally share our house and would periodically walk up the stares as if looking at someone at the top whilst being coaxed into the bedroom. Sarah Jenson could now leave this realm, now that her story had been told and in the following days she left us a pink and Lilac flower in our kitchen, pink and lilac were her favourite colours! The stepfather was also eventually removed but that was a hard fight which made the medium physically ill for a long time after the event.

This was to be my awakening that changed my life but also ended my career in the police, neither Sarah or I went back after this event.

From that point on I continued to see a multitude of unorthodox craft in our skies, ranging from 3 large cigar shaped UFO's just silently floating in the daylight sky above our home town, fire balls in the night sky, small controlled craft above the beach and sea on holiday, star looking objects in the night sky that just started moving in sync and even juxtapose craft in tandem at warp light speed, also at night. I have seen 2 dimensional gateways opening up, the first being at night when a wormhole suddenly appeared in the night sky after which a small craft emanated out of the end as it transited across the sky until it and the wormhole both disappeared a short time between. The second occasion I was walking through a dense forest near to my home with Sarah and a friend which I detail in a little while.

I was once telepathically invited to a certain location, just like the characters of the 1980's movie 'Close Encounters of the Third Kind' whereby again the area was littered with orbs, an image I was shown the previous night. And I have even stood next to a being not of this world whose presence altered my frequency and vibrations within! And one evening whilst at work as a police officer I was most likely on the centre of a UFO landing of some kind with lots of reports of silhouettes in back gardens which weren't there when we arrived and whilst we were there further reports were coming of figures in the as we were outside and yet again there was nothing to be seen. This was at the same time of numerous electrical explosions underground which had the local electricity board scratching their heads!

The evening was like this:

A night filled of dark matter sporting pockets of eternal light above me, but it was clear and unusually charged like the jousting lance of a brave knight on the back of his loyal stallion. This was to be an unorthodox evening to rival any other that had manifested before it. Parade over I boarded my police vehicle with my wife as passenger for a night shift with a difference. *"Mobile 30 (my police vehicle call sign) can you make an intruder alarm...?"*, the radio crackled and the controller's voice came through giving the location. On my way from not too far away, but what will I find there, is it a genuine alarm call, or is it just a regular false alarm?

First to arrive, but nothing amiss, at ground level at least. With other officers present I looked to the sky, a flash of light caused by two juxtaposed shooting stars travelling faster than the blink of my eyes, but these were not shooting stars as their odyssey turned them into warped luminescent dots, a scene from star-trek in my vicinity and not my TV screen. An eerie feeling hung around the air, we are not in control tonight there is something much bigger in town, a presence that gave us the shivers. Mobile 30 can you attend intruders in a rear garden, the radio crackles again, the same area and I'm on my way as street lights turn off I arrive again, no-one in the garden at all, but the caller is adamant, figures have been seen in the garden walking around. One final look and nothing in sight we leave but as we reached the street outside the callers house, another call comes through from the same person, the intruders are back! But there was nothing again, impossible for an escape we were already there just feet away.

Other calls of an exact nature are now coming in, in the area, but too far away for it to be the same people. The exact same scenario, intruders in the garden, officers arrive, no one there, they leave and further calls are received to say the intruders/silhouettes are back. Now street lights are turning off, the whole area spanning for miles is pitch black, the sounds of explosions caused by electrical charges are heard all around us one after the other like bombs activating. Then the most deafening of sounds, a manhole cover is blown out of the road as its circular metal cover, reminiscent of a UFO disc itself, flies through the air but landing safely a short distance away. Now the atmosphere can be cut by a knife, we are definitely not in control here. Inner senses are stirring like a whirlwind as they detect outsider presences as my energy field meets the dimensionally invisible but my radar has made contact. The electricity board confirmed that they had had 9 underground sub-station explosions that evening which is totally out of the ordinary as they usually expect one if that! An evening of call after call, incident after incident, with nothing to show for it other than the scene from a disaster movie.

Shift over and it's 7am and we're on our way home arriving soon after. Sitting at our laptop we contacted a local UFO group by email who because of our regular sightings we had spoken to several times before. We detail all that had happened that night but as we did so our emails disappeared from their folder only to be returned several minutes later like they had been removed copied and then put back, as we witnessed each stage of this process. We had experienced things like this before with the bugging of our landline phone and our mobiles as they began to tap activated by certain key words during personal conversations, confirmed by a phone engineer who found a strange device in the main telephone wire box outside our house, Government Communications Headquarters, GCHQ, a likely culprit.

The UFO group also investigated and spoke with the electricity board who confirmed the same information to them. I have seen on many occasions craft of electromagnetic space propulsion, riding of electrical currents, the best shapes to do so being a disc and a tube. I have seen their single magnetic polarity and negative mass and I have seen their craft piloted by thought. And for those of you who are familiar with Roswell and the none Earthly metal that was found at the crash site that no matter what they did always returned to its original shape and mass, well that's molecular programming at work! The lights emanated by their craft are the result of electromagnetic disturbances as both colour and light are frequencies within an electromagnetic field.

Take your mind back to the 80's movie ET, the landing, the crew disembarking their craft and scurrying around the area on that star-lit night. What if that location had been densely populated, just think how many calls the local police would have received that night, intruders in the garden following unusual activity in the skies. I no longer have to think as I look back on my former career, I have been amongst it and there is a power greater than we know just a micron away, not in a galaxy far far away but a mere frequency outside of our own.

Another one of many such incidents is what I term 'My Rendlesham Forest': The Dimensional Portal. A 17 year experienced ex-Police Officer with a keen eye for detail with my wife and friend walking through a dark and unlit park near to our home. A walk and track that we had taken many times before, not always without incident, but nothing like what was about to happen. No cars present, no people present other than ourselves and no street lights present at all. We had taken many photographs of the area around us that night as we felt something following us, the photographs confirmed the presence of an unusually high concentration of Orbs! Some containing what are known as 'Rods'. But nevertheless we continued on our track as the night drew in faster and faster! We had been invited to places prior to this night, prompted and influenced to attend a certain place at a certain time like the characters from 'Close

Encounters of the Third Kind' by an unknown force...

We had seen craft above us in broad daylight and at night previously and a few years after had actually stood next to a being not of this world! And we had been at the centre of a possible landing whilst at work as police officers! But tonight was just as special.

As we walked through the dense park a light appeared from nowhere in front of us (Nowhere meaning 'Now Here') so bright that it hurt our eyes to look directly at it. The mass of pure white light was at ground level raising about 20 feet into the air, amongst the trees, and about 15 feet ahead of us! But unlike Rendlesham Forest, this didn't appear to be a craft it appeared to be a dimensional gateway/portal to another place. There was no sound, just a silent stillness lasting about a minute or so until the light simply disappeared as fast as it had arrived restoring the park back to normality and complete darkness. As we frantically moved around my wife's mobile phone, which was in her hand, seemingly took a photograph of the light by itself as she did not press the button to do so herself! As the darkness returned the questions were endless, this had happened to us once before but that was a wormhole in the night sky that had enabled a craft to emanate out of it and travel across the night sky before our very eyes also, but this was at ground level and in front of our path. This was my Rendlesham Forest incident and will remain with me, with us all, for eternity!

There are many more events such as visitations of electromagnetic forces (angels) and other worldly visitors. In fact there are too many to actually mention here. I have even seen the spirit of a certain character of historical Royalty from the English civil war, namely King Charles I. The English Civil Wars (1642-1651) stemmed from conflict between Charles I and Parliament over an Irish insurrection. The first war was settled with Oliver Cromwell's victory for Parliamentary forces at the 1645 Battle of Naseby. The second phase ended with Charles' defeat at the Battle of Preston and his subsequent execution in 1649. Charles' son, Charles, then formed an army of English and Scottish Royalists, which prompted Cromwell to invade Scotland in 1650. The following year, Cromwell shattered the remaining Royalist forces and ended the "wars of the three kingdoms," though Charles II eventually ascended to the throne in 1660. Then long after the event has been written into the history books and the shelves of numerous libraries a remnant appears in the 21st century in front of my eyes.

I live in the ancient capital of Mercia but in modern times, yet time has travelled from the 17th Century England to greet me now! One evening, whilst within a local meeting place, I looked up and saw the spirit of King Charles 'I' walking out of a room through the door and across the room I was sitting in. The King just looked straight at me as I looked straight at him, no words spoken between us, just eye contact for that brief moment when time merged. His appearance was accompanied by a pungent smell, so combined this was the activation of several mediumship senses, namely third eye vision and smell (Clairolfaction which is psychic smell). Charles was wearing a burgundy cavalier suit and a matching burgundy cavalier hat as he simply vanished back into the realms beyond my five senses. The moment lasted less than a minute but the memory of it will last forever, a brush with English Royalty from days gone by. Just what must he have been thinking as he saw me sitting there in modern attire looking at him?

(King Charles 'I')

Time and reality is far more than we understand or know and has far more facets than we often realise. This was one evening when the past walked passed!

The paranormal is often a daily occurrence for me. I have seen green coloured grids in a funnel shape coming from the bottom of the Moon and numbers in the sky instead of clouds. I have heard what the Native American Indians called 'Voices of the wind' and there is so much more that I could have written about and discussed. I have even seen electromagnetic forces (known as angels) causing controlled energy explosions as they entered the room to then manifest as giant orbs of differing colours before shooting off at warp speed leaving only a trail of light as they exit the room.

We are not the only living existence in this universe and we are not the only living existence on our own planet!

And now going back to the 'being' not of this world, having stood a little more than 3 feet away from him in broad daylight as he just walked passed us. His energy field made me spin like a washing machine internally, I was with Sarah and a friend at the time who also felt the same way energetically. He was about 6'3" tall, pale and gaunt with stretched skin as if it had been forced over the bones and contours of his face and his hair was greyish and looked as if it was a hundred years old, it was thin like a fibre wire and below the collar line. Sarah and our mutual friend, both had their own experience with this 'man'.

(A sketch of what we saw)

Once we realise that we are not alone and a big part of the whole we can again start to see ourselves as part of a galactic community but there are those who try and stop this information coming out and try and create a false reality for people and in the next chapter I will detail who they are! Welcome to my world...

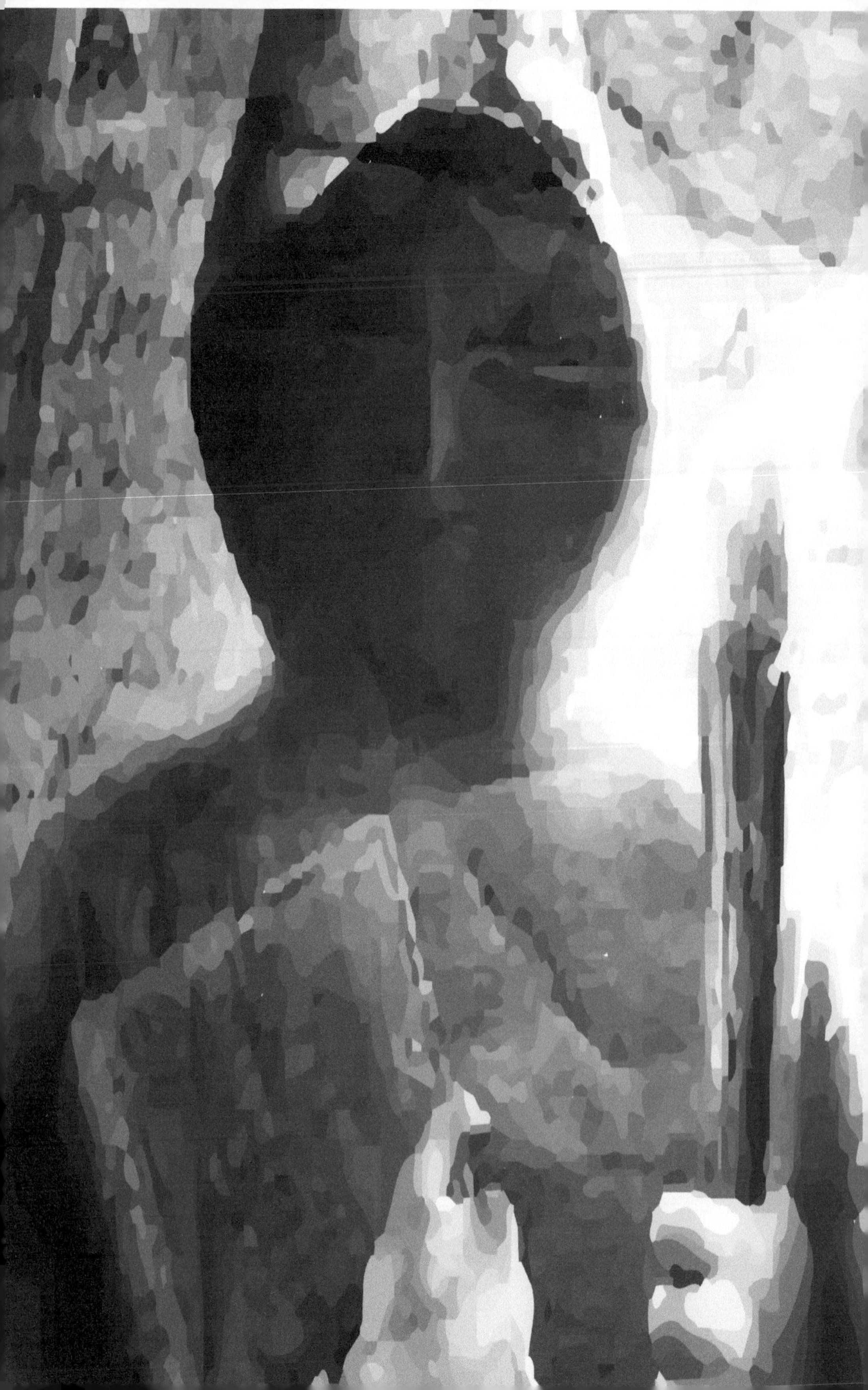

4

The Ego Of Man: When Knowledge Became Concealed

Having heard of just a few of my own personal experiences it is clear that there is a lot going on beyond the limitations of our frequency spectra. But certain powers that be don't want people to realise this. In this chapter I going to cite certain groups who wish to keep these things a secret and in subsequent chapters I will reveal many mysteries that have perplexed scholars and alike for many hundreds if not thousands of years. These mysteries and secrets are the ancient code that this book refers to. I will reveal just who the biblical characters such as Jesus Christ and Mary Magdalene really were and many of the other famous biblical characters, why the Pyramids of Egypt and Stonehenge were built and their purpose and I will also reveal who and what King Arthur was and even Santa Claus plus many more ancient mysteries. And most importantly what they actually mean!

Even the modern day Disney phenomenon has this secret code with the likes of the film Frozen with the main character Elsa on the North Mountain. Elsa means 'She Knows' (knowledge) and the North Mountain is the North gate, where the Pineal gland, the seat of consciousness, is situated within the human brain. With the re-emergence of Disney and a set of animated films such as the Little Mermaid, Frozen and many others which are again hitting the minds of Children and adults alike just who was Walt Disney and what were his motives? It is quite clear that Disney films have many subliminal messages of sex and low moral standards which speak to our sub-conscious mind. For many people who are familiar with Bloodline ruling families you will know that there are apparently 13 of them. But from those 13 families there are also other families who are interconnected and the Disney line is one of them (Merovingian). Walt means 'Ruler' and Disney derives from D'Insigny. The Disney family (originally D'Insigny) came to the UK with William the Conqueror with the Norman invasion of England. Walt Disney was a 33rd Degree Mason and was therefore privy to secret knowledge.

The global population has for far too long been fed a façade and an allegory, a story with a hidden meaning and it is about time that people understood what these widely celebrated events really signify and who and what they have been fooled into worshipping. Our lives are programmed and restricted to the point that our very existence is controlled by a contract. We are deliberately kept in a third dimensional low vibrational state of being and there are many ways in which this is being committed against us. The lives of our children and ourselves are seemingly pre-ordained and set out to a set program of how to behave and what to believe and what social standards to follow! But those expectant standards are created for us. We have become more or less cybernetic and controlled from the outside and we have allowed this to happen, inch by inch and foot by foot.

Throughout this book you will read a lot about consciousness and frequency under the term hertz, hertz being the amount of oscillations per second. The discovery of this has historically been attributed to Heinrich Hertz who was a German physicist who expanded the electromagnetic theory of light pioneered by Michael Faraday, and later by Maxwell. He is best-known for Hertz (Hz) unit of frequency per second cycle. However it was known and understood by ancient cultures which you will also read about as we venture through the chapters, so therefore he was not the one to discover it.

In order to understand Consciousness it is defined and described as follows: *Consciousness is the state or quality of awareness, or, of being aware of an external object or something within oneself. It has been defined variously in terms of sentience, awareness, qualia, subjectivity, the ability to experience or to feel, wakefulness, having a sense of selfhood or soul, the fact that there is something "that it is like" to "have" or "be" it, and the executive control system of the mind. In contemporary philosophy its definition is often hinted at via the logical possibility of its absence, the philosophical zombie, which is defined as a being whose behaviour and function are identical to one's own yet there is "no-one in there" experiencing it.*

And when I speak of 'Enlightened Consciousness' that means to 'transcend' normal awareness and in therefore an advancement of consciousness, as defined above.

But before I move onto frequency in this chapter I just wanted to highlight a few of the groups who decided amongst themselves that certain information and knowledge should be retained for themselves and not for general circulation. They created stories and allegories to achieve a smoke-screen and a lack of true focus, taking our eyes off their game. It is the Gnostic principle of concealment for the masses and knowledge for the worthy. If you control the highways and you wish to prevent someone's journey ending at a certain destination you simply litter that highway with diversion signs to alter the route taken. This is exactly what is happening, the people of global society have been cleverly diverted off the true track and have been deliberately sent the wrong way.

The first group that I will discuss are the Pharisees, a Jewish sect who believed themselves to be of greater sanctity and holiness than everyone else. The word Pharisee means to 'detach' or to 'separate' which is quite relevant.

The Pharisees are the spiritual fathers of modern Judaism. Their main distinguishing characteristic was a belief in an Oral Law that God gave to Moses at Sinai along with the Torah. The Torah, or Written Law, was akin to the U.S. Constitution in the sense that it set down a series of laws that were open to interpretation. The Pharisees believed that God also gave Moses the knowledge of what these laws meant and how they should be applied. This oral tradition was codified and written down roughly three centuries later in what is known as the Talmud. It is also widely believed that they created the dual Catholic Church which was also infiltrated by Crypto-Zionist Jews. Debt and a controlling monetary system has become the modern day chains of slavery and the world is under Maritime law, the law of commerce which is controlled by the Vatican bank which in itself is controlled by Zionist bankers. Even our legal systems are really there to enforce maritime law and not justice for the individual.

We are all Convicts of this legal system by way of being a Victim of a Con! It is no more than a church ecclesiastical system (Reminiscent of the Spanish Inquisition, Inquisition = period of prolonged questioning) stemming from Maritime Law and many of the legal terms give this clue. State your Name = NA-ME = No divine law, you are being Prosecuted = Pros-Se-Cutis = Skin, you are representing your own skin. We are referred to as ships under this Maritime law too with such words and phrases as relation-ship or a business partner-ship or an apprentice-ship and many others.

This stems from Cestie Que Vie Trusts of the Vatican Church (who run maritime/Cannon law) enforced in the 'Dock' by the Bench = Banco = Bank (commerce law). You have been Charged, and a charge relates to money, or even an electrical charge which is a current (Currency). Money is a great control system. We have all seen the curse of debt or even know someone close who has too. The modern day chain of slavery is debt. The threatening letters and visits from the bailiffs and pending prosecution soon follows for many, sleepless nights and constant worry and fear! But have you ever had letter after letter stating that your debts have been sold to a debt recovery agency? Well I hope so!

Not many people know this but debt recovery agencies actually only pay £10 for every £1000 of your debt, therefore if your debt is £3000 they have purchased it for just £30 from your original lender or even another debt recovery agency who have themselves at some point also purchased it and anything after that £30 investment and so on is clear profit for them! (It varies depending on the debt amount). Sickening, especially bearing in mind that it is the religious duty of Zionist bankers to charge the goyim as much interest as possible on loans! It is all a gigantic scam!

But there is a way out of it. And that is because of what's pinnacle in this (not bringing the strawman and signatures etc into this) is that you do not have a signed agreement or contract with the debt recovery agency that purchased your debt! They have in effect cleared your debt for you and have paid up your original lender! So thank you. And even more pinnacle is a section of British law, namely section 77A (6) of the Consumer Credit Act 1974 that states that because the debt recovery agency who purchased your debt does not have the correct paperwork (IE signed contract/agreement with you) you don't owe them anything and this is un-enforceable by them! (There will be the equivalent outside of the UK).

So next time these letters arrive just think and ask them for your contract where you agreed to pay them anything! There are also many get out of debt free websites online too.

Criminal how do you plea? = Cri-men = screams of distress (plea = emotional appeal) Crime = Sinfulness! Even the British police uniform is a shrine of masonic and Judaic kabbalah symbols. Police insignia has many hidden symbols and meanings not known to the public or even the police themselves, and I can state that as fact from experience. But let's take just one example the police helmet badge, the 7 pointed star, the Heptagram. The Heptagram is the symbol of the Kabbalah (Hebrew: הְלָבַּקָ‎, meaning "receiving/tradition") it is the Seal of Babylon, the Binah which means Understanding (bear in mind the police caution which asks at the end "Do you understand" in other words do you stand under?). The Binah is part of the Sephirot, the Hebrew Tree of Life and stands below the Keter meaning Crown. Look on the British police badge and you will see that the Binah is below the Keter (Crown) on the badge itself and is a representation of the Sephirot.

Judaism is also responsible for the vile and traumatic experience called circumcision, that may damage a child mentally forever, is a practice that the sane and rational mind would never do. It is totally immoral. But we are dealing with religious minds and they are often poisoned beyond reconciliation, poisoned to the verge of insanity and even beyond that! We are told that circumcision is for hygiene and medical reasons, but it isn't! So what is its origin? The origin is in the Hebrew scriptures regarding a character called Lilith who had a fall out with Adam and fled from Eden, she was the proto-type of Eve (this is their version not mine). Lilith is however the 'Lunar Apogee' which is when the Moon is furthest away from Earth and is known as the 'Dark Moon'. She was allowed to remain isolated and a witch and the mother of all demons and to kill infants up until their naming day, 7 days for girls and 8 days for boys. The circumcision of boys occurs on the 8th day after birth, which is no coincidence! The act and practice of circumcision is really a ritual to appease Lilith and her blood thirsty desire to do harm.

I could go on but in a nutshell we are from Birth (Berth, docking station for a ship) to death, Corpus, a dead entity, a business owned by the state (Vatican Trusts).

We have right of usage but we own nothing, they own it all under their contrived legal system, held in Lex Fori (law of the forum) Roman/Vatican Law (forum = COURTyard where justice and business was addressed).

In the 1500's the Roman Catholic Church, which is in itself a fake Christian front, created what is known as the Cestie Que Vie trust, in effect placing the whole planet in their control by means of that trust, by a 'Right of Claim' never challenged. Cestie Que Vie means 'For those who live'. It is symbolised by the 'Papal Tiara' the 3 tiered Crown (Vatican Crown). It controls Maritime law which is the law of the land and sea and claims owner-ship (Ship = a sea/water reference) of all persons, property and salt of the Earth.

(3 Tiered Crown of the Cestie Que Vie Trust)

Even the United States of America is really a corporation acting under Lex Fori (Law of the Forum – which is Roman Law) under the Potus (President) acting as 'Vassal King' (holder of land) answerable to the British Monarchy who are themselves answerable to the Vatican. The Pope's title is Vicarious Fili Dei which means 'In Place of the Son Of God'. They created 3 trusts,

(1) (Unum Sanctum- Crown of the land) When a child is born he/she loses

all benefits/entitlements and rights to land upon birth.

(2) (Aeterni Regis – Eternal Crown) When a child is born their birth certificate is sold as a bond (legally enforceable) to the private central bank of the nation of birth and they therefore lose all right to their flesh condemning them to perpetual servitude as a slave.

3) The 3rd Crown of the Ecclesiastical See (sea): When a child is Baptised parents are handing over the child's soul to the Vatican therefore removing the child's right over their own soul and denying them the right to stand as a person only a creature/thing without soul (Lost at sea) which is called 'Gift of Title of the soul' the 'Baptismal Certificate' which is then held in the Vatican vaults.

And without legal title over your own soul you will be denied legal standing and will be treated as things—cargo without souls—upon which the BAR (legal term for British Accreditation Registry) is now legally able to enforce Maritime law. The whole legal system is enforcing these trusts and our courts are enforcing Ecclesiastical/Cannon law as they did in the Spanish Inquisition and all to keep you and me in fear and in a low vibration.

The next group are the Sadducees.

The Sadducees were elitists who wanted to maintain the priestly caste, but they were also liberal in their willingness to incorporate Hellenism into their lives, something the Pharisees opposed. The Sadducees rejected the idea of the Oral Law and insisted on a literal interpretation of the written Law, consequently, they did not believe in an afterlife, since it is not mentioned in the Torah. The main focus of Sadducee life was rituals associated with the Temple. The Sadducees disappeared around 70 A.D, after the destruction of the Second Temple.

None of the writings of the Sadducees has survived, so the little we know about them comes from their Pharisaic opponents. These two "parties" served in the Great Sanhedrin, a kind of Jewish Supreme Court made up of 71 members whose responsibility was to interpret civil and religious laws.

And then we have the Essences.

A third faction was the Essenes who emerged out of disgust with the other two. This sect believed the others had corrupted the city and the Temple. They moved out of Jerusalem and lived a monastic life in the desert, adopting strict dietary laws and a commitment to celibacy. The Essenes are particularly interesting to scholars because they are believed to be an offshoot of the group that lived in Qumran, near the Dead Sea. In 1947, a Bedouin shepherd stumbled into a cave containing various ancient artefacts and jars containing manuscripts describing the beliefs of the sect and events of the time.

The most important documents, often only parchment fragments that had to be meticulously restored, were the earliest known copies of the Old Testament. The bible is the division of the Hebrew Scriptures.

"May Peace Be With You" is a quote heard so many times at Church. So let's look at how much the Church wants peace!

The Vatican is one of the highest shareholders in Beretta, an arms company and the Church of England is a major shareholder in General Electric (GE) again a company that has a branch that deals in firearms and military equipment. And not forgetting our knock on the door friends Jehovah's witnesses who hold a large share hold in Rand-Cam another company that deals in military equipment. So when your priests shout peace and love ask them why they bless weapons that will be used to kill someone in support of the 'Military Industrial Complex' maybe even later that day. Words are empty without the appropriate actions and we have money at the helm not peace!

We live in a world that has reverse polarity in terms of consciousness, we live in a world that's completely insane and backwards for anyone except those who make it backwards because for them it is the right way around. The likes of the Pharisees are your modern day Zionists and Illuminati, the enlightened ones and so are the upper levels of the Freemasons. Zionists are more often than not Khazars and the Khazarian converts to Judaism with an agenda to achieve the promise land of Israel with a world capital of Jerusalem which we can see happening with current global politics with President Trump recently giving Jerusalem to Israel.

There has always been a Religious connection to Kings, politics and power, all go hand in hand both historically and in the modern day which is no different. Many American citizens do not know that in 1871 their constitution was superseded by Lex Fori (Law of the Forum) which is Roman Vatican Law, and the Potus (President, which also means Celebrant of Eucharist/Holy Communion) is Vassal King, holder of land answerable to the British Monarchy who in turn are answerable to the Vatican. Rome has a senate in Capitoline Hill and America has a senate in Capitol Hill! Both have the Eagle as their symbol, the word America also means 'Rule of the eternal Eagle or the eternal Eagle's rule'. America is a corporation and Mr Trump is now CEO of that corporation.

The masons at the lower levels, the first 3 degrees, have a certain knowledge base but a lot is also kept from them by the higher levels of Freemasons. The word mason, although we are told originates from them being stonemasons actually comes from the two words of Mother-Son, which gives us an abbreviation of Ma'son = Mason. This is because of their focus of worship Sirius 'A' is believed to be the mother of our own solar sun and is the cosmic egg, this being the original Mary and Jesus (Isis & Horus in Egypt).

The solar Sun and Sirius 'A' are in a binary together and due to the 'Doppler Effect' when Sirius is moving away from Earth is it Red in colour and when it is on its return it is Blue, this is the Red and Blue star Kachina prophecy of the Hopi Indians. The Doppler Effect is the change in frequency or wavelength of a wave (or other periodic event) for an observer moving relative to its source and the star colour charts it is caused by such a change of frequency. Sirius 'A' has a frequency of 174 hertz which is the frequency that activates 'Super Consciousness'. The Masons call Sirius 'A' the 'Blazing star' as Sirius means 'Scorching'. Isis/Sirius 'A' is the goddess of Motherhood and when we see the Sun looking motif in masonic lodges that is really Sirius 'A'.

The word mother comes from Mitochondrion and other and the

Mitochondrion (plural Mitochondria) is a double membrane-bound organelle found in all eukaryotic organisms. Mitochondrial DNA (mtDNA) is passed on only through the mother and provides energy for the survival of a cell. Mitochondria supply cellular energy by generating adenosine triphosphate (ATP) which is used as a source of energy for the cells. Mitochondria are also involved in other tasks such as cellular differentiation, cellular signalling, cell growth and cell death. This is also relevant in the Biblical plagues of Egypt in the death of the first born which I will go into later in the Biblical chapters.

When you reach the 3rd level of freemasonry you can choose between the York rite of freemasonry which is more attuned to Christianity and the Scottish rite of freemasonry which is attuned to ancient Egypt. The name Scottish rite came from the Egyptian Queen Meritamun also known as Scotia (Scotland) who was the sister of King Tutankhamun and the daughter of Akhenaten and Nefertiti. It is believed that she came to the British Isles and later created the Irish Royal lineage, of which I am a descendant and also named the country Scotland after herself.

The highest public known levels of freemasonry is the 33rd degree, so why this number? As many of you will know the number 33 is a power number but it goes much deeper than that into the esoteric word. It just so happens that Jesus died aged 33, this is no coincidence, it is symbolic in this case, as you will see later, of the death or the end of the Earthly consciousness prior to its ascension to the heavenly consciousness, the crown of thorns! There are 33 vertebrae's in the human spine and at the top of our spine we get the skull, Golgotha, where our consciousness resides. 33 Hertz is the frequency of 'Christ Consciousness' and also it is the hertz frequency in sync with geometry, hence why we have the letter 'G' within the compass of masonic emblems. Also in Churches you will see the IHS symbol of Jesus which has 32 rays plus Christ in the centre which gives us 32+1 =33 (33 hertz).The numerical equivalent of 'amen' is also 33, 1 + 13 + 5 + 14 = 33. 'Amen' comes from 'amun' which means hidden. A = 1, M = 13, E = 5 and N = 14.

(Geometry of Divinity = GOD)

The word geometry means 'Earth measure' and the root letters of the word geometry are GMT which just so happens what we use as an abbreviation for London time under the phrase 'Greenwich Mean time'. Mean is a calculated central and Greenwich Mean Time is measured from 0 degrees longitude and 0 degrees latitude.

The masons know this deep esoteric truth at its higher levels and they see their work as the 'Great work'. This is also relevant in the religious masonic created Jehovah's witnesses who when they knock on your door trying to convert you into their belief they call it 'The work'. This is because their founder Charles Taze-Russell was a 33rd degree mason. Masonry is a Jewish establishment and how many people know that Britain is under the rule of Judaism? When we look at British culture and analyse its origins we can see that it comes from a Judaic faith and influence which in turn was influenced by ancient Egypt.

Our reigning Monarchy claim to be from the 'Royal House of David' and have connections to the tribe of Judah (Judah meaning young Lion) hence why the Lion is symbolic for British Royalty.

In biblical legend Jacob was visited on his pillow, known as Jacobs Pillow which is the coronation stone upon which Monarchs are crowned, and he was told that his seed would rule the world as Kings and Queens until the return of the Promised Land, Israel. Jacob was to later be called Israel. The British flag is called the 'Union Jack' which is the Union of Jacob from whom the 12 tribes of Israel were born. The Union of Jacob is the reconnection of the 12 tribes of Israel. The word British derives from 'B'nai B'rith' which means 'Man of the Contract' and that contract is with the Hebrew God Yahweh. The British National Anthem is 'God save the Queen' which again has these connotations. The Union Jack also has Egyptian significance too. So when you see Britain in all its glory and you hear the Queen's speech telling us all that we are a Christian nation bear in mind that they don't believe that for one minute. Bear in mind that they do not subscribe to what they are saying and that they have a different agenda and have a different belief system to the one they portray. Our legal system is Judaic, our Monarchy is Judaic and our banking system is Judaic and the global agenda of politics is one of Zionism, the return of the promised land of Israel.

The world of religion and secret societies is now mainly male dominated but this was not always the case. We lost the balance along the way and these institutions became male dominated, the brotherhoods, who today are involved in world 'Think-Tanks' forging global political policy. The world was once under a matriarchal system of balance, the divine feminine and Moon worship, which lead to the fertility cults, globally and of course in ancient Egypt. In Egypt the fertility cults involved the Goddess of motherhood, Isis. The Moon has an orbit frequency of 421 hertz, which is the frequency that speeds up spiritual development, which is the same frequency as the spin of the planet Mercury. Even the Church is representing the Moon in many ways, firstly the letters UR found within the word Church means Moon. The Moon reflects the light of the Sun and in astronomy the heavenly Christ is the solar Sun, therefore the Church is reflecting the light/knowledge of the Christ.

There are two types of archways on a Church which are the standard singular arch which represents the Sun but there is another type of arch called the 'Lunette' arch.

(Lunette Arch)

Lunette means Lunar which means Moon. The Lunette arch represents the 4 gates of the vagina, namely:

Labia

Clitoris

G-Spot

Womb

The female genitalia is known as the gate of heaven and it is the 'Holy

Grail', (the Grail is the womb) deriving from Graal meaning Vessel of God, a vessel being a place where the likes of blood is contained, it is the continuation of life. The wine drank from the Grail is menstrual blood, containing Moon energies. The area between the endocervix and ectocervix is known as the 'transformation zone' and those who drink from the grail are said to transform spiritually. Menstrual blood is the fountain of life and it activates stem cell capacity and consciousness and transports us to our endocrine state. In Church they sing Hymns which comes from the word Hymen. The hymen is a membrane that surrounds or partially covers the external vaginal opening but Hymen is also the Greek God of weddings, where we do of course sing Hymns! We can also trace fertility cults back to the worship of the Egyptian Goddess Isis. Isis was associated with the Star Sirius 'A', but her cosmic appearance in the sky was the 'Moon'. In ancient Egypt, they had a talisman/amulet called the 'Tyet' which was a similar shape to the famous 'Ankh'.

(The Tyet Symbolic of Menstrual Blood)

Isis is symbolic of Motherhood and menstruation is the time when females are at child bearing age and female body is closely locked into Moon cycles and also with the creation of the lunar seed (female version of the solar Christ seed that I mention later in the Jesus chapter). There are also countless pictures of modern day celebrities covering one eye, this is purely a secret language. If they cover their right eye leaving the left eye exposed this is Isis symbology and worship and if it is vice versa it is Horus symbology and worship.

Churches are built with artful symmetry on energy lines for the best harmonics and reproduction of sound. Even the concept of Nunnery has Sirius 'A' and Lunar Moon connections which both have correlation to Isis. In Egypt the Primordial chaotic waters of creation (Primordial Mound) were called the 'Nun' referring to motherhood and fertility! The Goddess of motherhood and fertility is 'Isis' the 'superior Mother' (Mother Superior). The word and Nunnery term 'Sister' derives from the words 'Isis-Star which is 'Sirius 'A' (associated with Isis). Isis is also associated with the 'Moon' and Nuns live in a 'Monastery' deriving from Moon-aster, Moon-star! The female body is locked into these lunar cycles with menstruation, the 'Blood of Isis' the 'Tyet'. Or as Leonardo Da Vinci would secretly hide this fact within his famous painting the Mona Lisa, Mona – L'Isa = The Moon is Isis! The word Catholic, which hosts the concept of Nunnery, means 'Universal' which is within the domain of astronomy. There is a Sun and Moon marriage highly relevant within the cults of male and female fertility. The Sun and Moon are the origin of Boaz and Jachin of freemasonry. Church spires are male mast energy and phallic symbols (Obelisks).

According to the Bible, Boaz and Jachin were two copper, brass or bronze pillars which stood in the porch of Solomon's Temple, the first Temple in Jerusalem. According to Josephus in Antiquities of the Jews, Boaz stood on the left when entering Solomon's Temple, while Jachin stood on the right, and the two were made by Hiram Abiff the founder of freemasonry. When we hear a Church Bell, when made of bronze, it has a frequency of 1133 hertz as a principle tone and Bel (spelt with one L) is the God of Fire and the Sun, hence why a Bell is often golden, it represents the Sun, hence why the elites of the world are involved in a think tank called the

'Bilderberg Group' meaning God of the mountain (Sun God). Bilderberg = Bel who was the Phoenician Sun-God (Phoenicia is the modern day Syria that is being attacked now by western forces, it is also a part of the region known as 'Greater Israel) and the word Bilderberg combined means God of the Mountain and a mountain can represent a dwelling of a holy being/God. The God of the Mountain is El-Shaddai who is Yahweh and that mountain is 'Mount Zion' in Jerusalem, hence Zionist! The world has been infiltrated by Crypto-Jews who have the Zionist agenda in mind, the promised land of Israel, which they believe to be theirs by God right.

1133 is also the numerical code in gemetria, the numerical value of letters and words, of the Archangel Michael, who is the soul essence of the Sun and in the 4 elements he is the element of fire. According to Jehovah's witnesses the heavenly name for Jesus is Michael, ironic as both relate to the solar Sun. They are not the same entity but there is an obvious Sun connection between the two of them which is usually completely missed by many, especially those who claim to be of the 'truth'. The Sun in Hebrew is called Shamash which means servant, Jesus was God's servant!

In the Hindu religion they believed that the word/chant 'Om' was the primordial sound that created the universe. But Om is the Sun, as in the Judaic belief of Solomon which separated is Sol- Om-On, which is the word for the Sun in 3 different languages. Sol is Latin, Om is Hindu and On is Coptic Egyptian! So when we are at home and we turn the light ON, this is what we are really doing, shinning the light. The wavelength for the chant Om is 7.23cm ironically this is the exact distance between the chakras of the human body and also the distance between the human nose and chin!

But more about Jesus and the connection to the Sun in a later chapter.

The Sun has a frequency of 126 hertz which is the frequency of 'Unity Consciousness' and is the border between yin and yang and a transcendental frequency. The yin and yang symbol is the 6 and 9 the forces of chaos and order/creation in an electromagnetic gravitational dance, a duality, opposite poles. But there was a point in time where Patriarchal priesthoods began to assert their influence and sacred knowledge became hidden and concealed from the general population and retained for certain individuals within various sects. These sects believed themselves to be of higher sanctity than anyone else and became known as the elites, elite derives from el-lite meaning Gods chosen ones. This knowledge is our pathway out of the chains that hold us locked in a low vibration and the brotherhoods and priesthoods are blocking our way, erecting diversion signs that lead us away from the true path and into locations elsewhere. They do not want us follow the real path to our enlightenment and are deliberately blocking our way and our route.

It is time that we moved them aside...

5

The Third Dimensional Prison: Life Without Parole

So now you know who is behind the concealment of your rightful inheritance, namely knowledge, let me move onto how they are doing it to us, before I reveal the greatest deceptions in history in the following chapters! This is done in so many different ways but it works well, and well is a real understatement. Knowledge naturally advances our soul and consciousness so it is, at all costs, kept from us all. Another way they keep us within this prison of low vibration is also on a more physical level which combined with the metaphysical does a good all round job on us. Our body, as is the universe, is a vibratory vessel that can be influenced by outside things. For example most music worldwide has been tuned to 440 hertz since the International Standards Organization (ISO) endorsed it in 1953 whereas prior to this it was tuned to 432 hertz which is a harmonious mathematical tone in sync with the universe.

440 hertz is really a disharmony and an attack on the human subconscious. I will discuss the relevance of hertz and its connection to our consciousness later on in the book when I take you to Egypt to reveal its mysteries and decode its messages, but suffice to say for now sound is highly important. If our internal vibrations and frequencies are low it is much more difficult to connect to higher vibrations and frequencies and we can remain more isolated, something that these groups are fully aware of. Often low and high vibrations are not compatible with each other and will not connect. There is a theory that the change from 432 Hz to 440 Hz was dictated by Nazi propaganda minister, Joseph Goebbels. He used it to make people think and feel a certain manner, and to make them a prisoner of a certain consciousness. Then around 1940 the United States introduced 440 Hz worldwide, and finally in 1953 it became the ISO 16-standard. There is a belief that the Rockefeller Corporation also had an input into this.

In a paper entitled 'Musical Cult Control', Dr Leonard Horowitz writes: "The music industry features this imposed frequency that is 'herding' populations into greater aggression, psycho social agitation, and emotional distress predisposing people to physical illness". They knew exactly what they were doing when they altered the frequency of western music. The powers that be are successfully lowering the vibrations of not only the younger generation but the general population itself. These destructive frequencies entrain the thoughts towards disruption, disharmony and disunity. Additionally, they also stimulate the controlling organ of the body - the brain - into disharmonious resonance, which ultimately creates disease and war. Divide and conquer has always worked for them, just look at the curse called religion. We have become little more than worker ants scurrying around working for a Queen. We go out and work all day to pay for the house that we not in because we are out working and we then have our hard earned money stolen from us by a tax system run by threat and fear.

Music has a hidden power to affect our minds, our bodies, our thoughts, and our society. When that music is based upon a tuning standard purposely removed from the natural harmonics found in nature, the end result may be the psychic poisoning of the mass mind of humanity.

"If one should desire to know whether a kingdom is well governed, if its morals are good or bad, the quality of its music will furnish the answer."
– Confucius

Frequency and vibration hold a critically important yet hidden power to affect our lives, our health, our society and our world. The science of Cymatics (meaning the study of visible sound and vibration) proves that frequency and vibration are the master keys and organizational foundation for the creation of all matter and life on this planet. When sound waves move through a physical medium (sand, air, water, etc.) the frequency of the waves has a direct effect upon the structures which are created by the sound waves as they pass through that particular medium. Every chakra (energy wheel) within the human body has a hertz frequency as follows:

Crown – 216 / 432 / 864 Hertz – A (musical note tuning)

Third Eye – 144 / 288 / 576 Hertz – D (musical note tuning) (also the DNA double helix code)

Throat – 192 / 384 / 768 Hertz – G (musical note tuning)

Heart – 128 / 256 / 512 Hertz – C (musical note tuning)

Solar Plexus – 182 / 364 / 728 Hertz – F Sharp (musical note tuning)

Sacral – 303 / 606 / 1212 Hertz – E Flat (musical note tuning)

Root – 228 / 456 / 912 Hertz – B flat (musical note tuning)

The chakra system is important when we also talk in terms of consciousness and access to higher knowledge. The third eye (Pineal gland) diminishes with constant negativity, and our life is full of manufactured negativity which keeps us locked in the third dimension. I talk extensively about the pineal gland in later chapters.

Nikola Tesla once said *"Alpha waves in the human brain are between 6-8 hertz. The wave frequency of the human cavity resonates between 6-8 hertz. All biological systems operate in the same frequency range. The human brain's alpha waves function in this range and the electrical resonance of the Earth is between 6-8 hertz. Thus, our entire biological system – the brain and the Earth itself work on the same frequencies. If we can control that resonate system electronically we can directly control the entire mental system of humankind"* and he also said, *"If you could eliminate certain outside frequencies that interfered in our bodies, we would have greater resistance toward disease".* And by raising our bodily frequencies we can assist our immune systems to better fight and overcome disease.

Our DNA helixes are musical instruments that are constantly receiving MHz of electricity and the audial currents, which require sound. If that sound is dis-harmonic, a DNA starts to resonate to external dis-harmonics. Should the external resonating tune sources in a person of old age that has their DNA viruses resonating to the outside, become harmonic, then the DNA viruses will remember their coherent PHI-like spiral shape and possibly commence regeneration, Since 8 hertz in DNA replication has been described by Scientific American (March 1965, p 28), to be behaving as a room temperature superconductor, the use of sound may enable such genetic alchemy.

The average frequency of the human body during the daytime is 62-68

Hz. A healthy body frequency is 62-72 Hz. When the frequency drops, the immune system is compromised.

Human Body: (MHz = Megahertz = one million cycles per second)

Genius Brain Frequency 80-82 MHz
Brain Frequency Range 72-90 MHz
Normal Brain Frequency 72 MHz
Human Body 62-78 MHz
Human Body: from Neck up 72-78 MHz
Human Body: from Neck down 60-68 MHz Thyroid and Parathyroid glands are 62-68 MHz
Thymus Gland is 65-68 MHz
Heart is 67-70 MHz
Lungs are 58-65 MHz
Liver is 55-60 MHz
Pancreas is 60-80 MHz

Colds and Flu start at: 57-60 MHz
Disease starts at: 58 MHz
Candida (a genus of yeast) overgrowth starts at: 55 MHz
Receptive to Epstein Barr (human herpes virus) starts at: 52 MHz
Receptive to Cancer starts at: 42 MHz
Death begins at: 25 MHz

FOODS:

(fresh foods and herbs can be higher if grown organically and eaten freshly picked): (HZ = Hertz, oscillations per second)

Fresh Foods 20-27 Hz
Fresh Herbs 20-27 Hz
Dried Foods 15-22 Hz
Dried Herbs 15-22 Hz
Processed/Canned Food 0 HZ (the majority of food we eat).

Many pollutants lower healthy frequency. Processed/canned food has a frequency of zero. Fresh produce has up to 15 Hz, dried herbs from 12 to 22 Hz and fresh herbs from 20 to 27 Hz.

Essential oils start at 52 Hz and go as high as 320 Hz, which is the frequency of rose oil. Clinical research shows that therapeutic grade essential oils have the highest frequency of any natural substance known to man, creating an environment in which disease, bacteria, virus, fungus, etc., cannot live. And this is exactly what is happening, we are being made unwell by our manufactured environment.

This is what is meant by vibration and frequency.

VIBRATION DEFINITION: *"An oscillation of the parts of a fluid or an elastic solid whose equilibrium has been disturbed or of an electromagnetic wave or a person's emotional state, the atmosphere of a place, or the associations of an object, as communicated to and felt by others".*

FREQUENCY DEFINITION: *"Frequency is the number of occurrences of a repeating event per unit of time. It is also referred to as temporal frequency, which emphasizes the contrast to spatial frequency and angular frequency. The period is the duration of time of one cycle in a repeating event, so the period is the reciprocal of the frequency. For example, if a new-born baby's heart beats at a frequency of 120 times a minute, its period—the time interval between beats—is half a second. Frequency is an important parameter used in science and engineering to specify the rate of oscillatory and vibratory phenomena, such as mechanical vibrations, audio signals, radio waves, and light".*

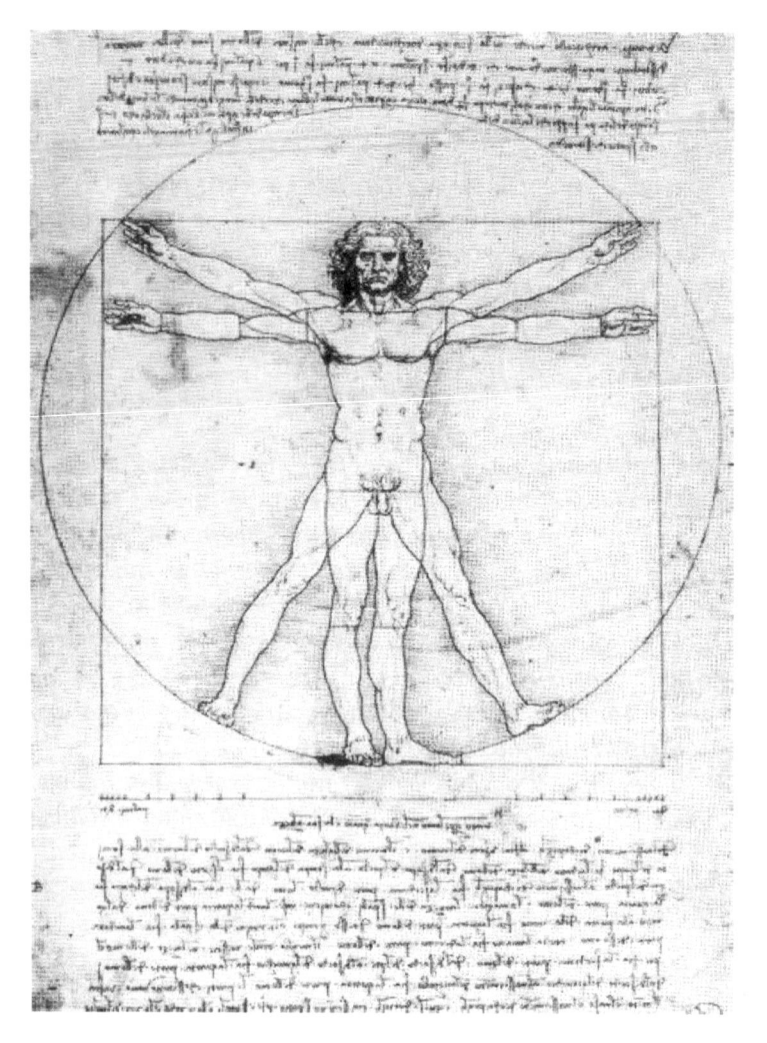

(Vitruvian Man)

Leonardo Da Vinci's Vitruvian man tells us estoterically of the 4 bodies of human vibrational existence which must all be balanced. The man is the physical body, the arms and legs are the dynamic stages of the emotional body, the box is the confined mind and the circle is the spiritual body. We have become the squared circle, the infinite brought down into the finite world.

YOUR PHYSICAL BODY:

Your physical body is the vessel that your spirituality, emotions and creativity flow through. The physical, emotional, mental and spiritual bodies are literal vibrational fields of energy that overlap and affect each other profoundly. The physical body has a great capacity to inform you when something is wrong or right. It can be positively or negatively affected by the foods we eat, the thoughts we think and the emotional state that we reside in at any given moment.

Feeling a situation as opposed to thinking about a situation is the way to properly use your physical body. This is the ultimate and intended use of the body, the heart will always express itself to you through your feeling/physical body. Learning to "feel" what your body is telling you and responding to those messages is the key to finding harmony and balance. This is the vibrational secret of the Vitruvian Man. You must learn to feel and understand the multitude of energy signatures or messages that your heart is sending through your physical body. In the modern day, people primarily live in their minds separating themselves from their physical body. Our cells energetically remember everything that has ever happened to you, good or bad, and influence the present.

YOUR EMOTIONAL BODY:

Your emotional body is the sum total of every emotional experience you have ever had and also your general concerns pleasures and desires. Did you know that the word 'emotion' means "energy in motion"? Where thoughts and feelings go, energy flows.

Hurtful experiences throughout life are energetically held as layers of memory (within the subconscious and unconscious mind) within the body that drive day-to-day thoughts and feelings. Therefore, if you are not aware of your inner wounds and have not healed these past wounds you become a prisoner to the negative energetic influences. Have you ever felt yourself exhibiting unwanted behaviours or reacting in a certain way that did not feel like your true self? These unwanted reactions are the result of emotional wounds that exist as contracted energy living within you and driving your behaviour.

Also residing within the emotional body is love. When something is right or good we feel the joyous moment our heart is communicating to us via our positive emotion. This is the desired state of being. Our life's purpose is the fulfilment of the heart. Honouring all that is positive, passionate, joyful and harmonious leads to this fulfilment. When we heal the layers of emotional wounds we then move ourselves to a predominate state of joy and love as opposed to experiencing it in fleeting moments.

YOUR MENTAL BODY:

The mental body is also a powerful, dynamic energy instrument. There are two parts to the mental body: the egoist mind (little mind) and the Divine mind. The egoist mind is a powerful tool for creating a harmonious reality or a reality of suffering. It was not meant to be the driving force of our existence, only a tool to be used to direct and achieve our expanded awareness. When its task of setting an intention or forming a desire is finished, which could be in a few seconds, we should then turn this tool off and return to residing within the feeling body. This gives way to experiencing or residing in Divine mind (I AM PRESENCE).

The vibrational experience of Divine mind begins as a subtle calming that deepens into the peace beyond understanding. When existing from Divine mind the constant mental churning is surrendered. However, in modern day, the programming of living within the egoist mind prevents this from happening. It is up to you to choose where you wish to reside – in the churning egoic mind or the peaceful Divine mind.

YOUR SPIRITUAL BODY:

The circle in the Vitruvian Man represents the spiritual body which is the infinite doorway to many high vibrational states of expanded awareness, enlightened awakening, and our mystical self. The secret of the four bodies of existence is that when the physical, mental and emotional bodies reach a state of harmony and balance, the higher vibration of our spiritual body is activated. Thus begins the ever increasing unfoldment of our spiritual nature that begins to open the doorway into enlightened and expanded states of consciousness. These states of expanded consciousness lead to the direct experience of the light of the soul or soul merging.

Throughout the history of humanity, this illuminated state has been lying dormant, waiting to be discovered. It has always been available to mankind. However, for millennium mans' inhumanity to man has perpetuated the prison of pain and suffering.

Leonardo Da Vinci spoke in codes, as do those in the know! And within the Vitruvian man are secrets to our enlightenment as with all of the other pieces of information portrayed within this book.

IN THE NEWS TODAY:

How often do we hear good news on our TV's, Radio or Newspapers? Not very often and again there is good reason for that, negative news has a negative effect on the body and our moods. Being surrounded by negativity plummets us into deep depression and even more negativity which keeps us at a low ebb and unable to lift ourselves sufficiently to want to fight, it knocks the wind from our sails and this way we are depressed and deflated, down and easily controllable. Every thought has the potential to change the chemistry of the body.

Our newspapers and media generally are controlled by very few people, hence why the newspaper central is in Fleet Street in London. Fleet means 'under the same ownership or control' and this is no mistake! And this is only a small part of the overall attack on humanity, there are many others.

GMO's (Genetically Modified Organisms) are added to food which cause harm and modify the body genetically from within, fluoride is added to water which is known to calcify and block the pineal gland from working correctly and effectively, and then we get the daily clusters of positive Ions from (Geoengineering/Chemtrails) which then become negative causing illness and lethargy when added to the air. Pharmaceutical companies and doctors flood our system with medication and Pharmacy derives from 'Pharmacia' who was a water nymph of the river of poison, it means sorcerery in other languages.

Technology has become a zombie like distraction, and as we saw in the Nikola Tesla quote it is also controlling our mental frequencies and taking us away from a connection of a greater kind but in the same breathe it is causing harmful illnesses. A recent study in Sweden suggested that acoustic neuromas (benign tumours of the acoustic nerve) are twice as common in mobile phone users as in those who do not use mobiles. And then of course we have the numerous radioactive masts dotted around the landscape.

And then we have the illusion of politics, the constant battle of left and right, the thing to remember here is that the left and right wing belong to the same bird! All in all the powers that be try everything in a multi-facetted attack on many fronts to keep us down and keep us at that low frequency.

Now I have briefly spoken about the system that's used against us and by whom I will now begin to reveal the secrets that have been deliberately kept from us, which once known will put humanity on a level playing field. So here are many of the ciphered codes and meanings that have been concealed from us for eons of time. You already know the mass production mainstream biblical accounts so I won't repeat the versions given to us by the Church and alike but in the following chapters I will tell you what they actually mean and your knowledge base will elevate as a result. You will now know what they know!

That way they lose their advantage...

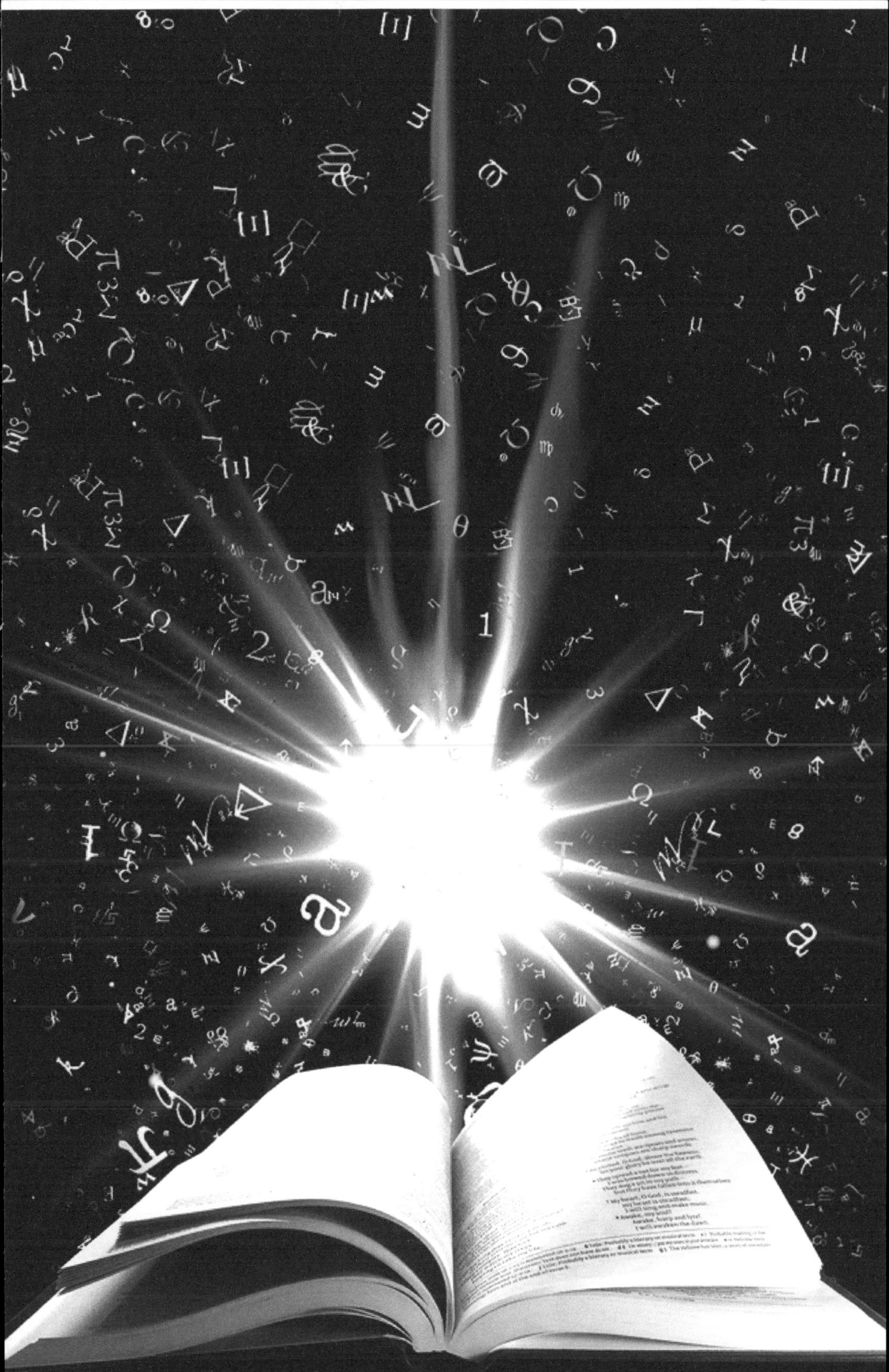

6

The Bible Code: What The Priesthoods Don't Want You To Know

Religion is a set of beliefs in a cosmic deity and depending upon which religion you follow, often a parental influence, will determine which god you worship. But little do the followers of various religions, (whom believe that their beliefs are correct and that no other religion is correct), know, is that all religions are simply different branches of the same tree planted by the aristocracy of days gone by, who created many different factions to cause confusion and division whilst holding onto the real meanings and truths for themselves. With so many religions claiming that they are the truth someone is going to be very disappointed!

As of 2014, there are an estimated 4,200 different religions in the world, and these can be categorized into several main religions. These include Christianity, Roman Catholicism, Islam, Hinduism, Buddhism and Judaism, although Roman Catholicism is often categorized under Christianity. So with so many different beliefs, which of them is the truth? Unless of course they all have the same point of origin and base which is the truth that has been cleverly hidden from us with the creation of stories and icons, then it is much easier to see what is the truth and that truth will be revealed to you in the forthcoming chapters. The tree is the truth yet the branches (the multiple religions) are the diversion away from the original bark of knowledge. There has been the creation of the canopy between human and God, by the introduction of priests and religious leaders, to teach falsity within religious buildings. The introduction of reward, everlasting life in heaven and punishment with the creation of a place called hell and the chains of sin, all to keep the followers imprisoned and handcuffed to a system of beliefs. Whilst all of the time knowing that these teachings are not correct and that these characters are a metaphor and an allegory for something much deeper.

I always knew when I saw the most wonderful of Churches that deep within the architecture, sermons, stained glass windows and the stories heard throughout my childhood and life there was a much deeper meaning. It was a language of codes that I began to understand and decipher and my feelings turned out to be correct. Their mystique spoke to me at my very essence, their symmetry and significant harmonic and sonic locations resonated with me. There is a double speak going on, one for the general public and the other for the initiates who have been given the knowledge

(Knowledge = to know). And there is a big difference between the two.

Religion has tainted the minds of billions of people around the world and has achieved its main goals, to fool us and deceive us and to keep us all from the real target as we are chasing and relying upon the icons of salvation. They are not coming and they are not coming because we are looking outside of ourselves for them when really they are within us. They control by fear or reward, the reward of heaven or the punishment of hell failing to mention that hell derives from helig meaning holy place and originates from Egypt and the underworld ruled by Osiris who judged the soul. And this will become apparent by the end of this book.

I have found a code that is a blueprint that spans all across the whole ancient world and is a secret code that connects them all in a deep way! And that code is genetic, which is the study of genes, genetic variation, and heredity in living organisms. It is generally considered a field of biology, but intersects frequently with many other life sciences and is strongly linked with the study of information system. In the following chapters I am about to discuss that code covering the most famous biblical characters and stories who are revered throughout the world.

The first scripture of the Bible is Genesis and Genesis means the beginning but the word Genesis derives from the phrase the 'Gene of Isis' or 'Genetics of Isis' which is very pinnacle in deciphering the bible code! Isis was the Goddess of Motherhood, the cosmic womb, in ancient Egypt. Isis means she of the throne and she is the Pituitary gland which is the seat/throne of the mind.

John 1:1 is the first verse in the Gospel of John. The King James Version of the verse reads, "In the beginning was the Word, and the Word was with God, and the Word was God". This is setting the scene for creation but just what is the word? This is referring to human genetics. Human genetics have 4 nucleotides namely Adenine, Thymine, Guanine and Cytosine. Nucleotides are organic molecules that serve as the monomer units for forming the nucleic acid polymers deoxyribonucleic acid and ribonucleic acid, both of which are essential biomolecules in all life-forms on Earth. Nucleotides are the building blocks of nucleic acids, they are composed of three subunit molecules: a nitrogenous base, a five-carbon sugar, and at least one phosphate group. They are also known as phosphate nucleotides. The letters of the 4 nucleotides have 64 combinations acting as a genetic language and an internal alphabet. In basic gemetria which is the numerical value of letters and words the number 64 is God! These are the building blocks of life, the genesis pattern, as the embryo develops in sequences of 8 until it reaches the '64' tetrahedron grid which is full development.

'In the beginning was the word and the word was with God and the word was God' and to end the parable and to add my own conclusion to that sentence in order to state what it really should have said, 'The word is DNA', that in numerical value is God!

The code I have deciphered throughout the Bible is the workings of DNA and as you will see I have attributed all of the most famous biblical stories and events to the inner workings of the human body and its genetic system, the universe within us. Genetics is a hidden universe within that we hardly ever think or even see. We are taught less about this than the cosmic universe and yet it is our very essence. The bible starts off with genetics and it doesn't stop there, is it the hidden theme throughout.

So in the next chapter I will decode and decipher the 'Adam and Eve' story.

ב

Adam & Eve And The Garden Of Eden: The Inner Body

Imagine being the first two human beings on a new Earth that satisfied God. No noise, no stress, no illness, no age increases and a blissful and innocent existence. No rain as water came from a canopy and dome above the planet, which was under perfect climate control. If the bible is to be believed Adam and Eve were enjoying a fulfilling relationship with themselves and with their creator. Work was an enjoyment and not a tax paying chore which allowed for a day of rest on the Sabbath. All in all it would seem a perfect paradise on Earth. But all was about to change and doom humanity into a life of sin and death for eons to follow. Eve was tempted by the serpent and she ate the fruit from the tree of knowledge. This was the turning point in human history. But this is a biblical version of the entrance of man and woman onto God's Earth and it is not real!

I have for this biblical story and all of the other most famous stories and characters attributed the Adam and Eve story to the workings of human genetics.

Let's start with the famous Apple of temptation. An apple is associated with knowledge and an allusion which is a figure of speech, but most of all it is an allegory, a story with a hidden meaning. When we introduce the serpent into the story we are really talking about knowledge and wisdom which is being denied the masses, the coiled serpent energy of Kundalini spiritual awakening of our third eye, it is the forbidden fruit which is the Pineal gland (pinecone and pine nut which is a fruit) and only the chosen can have access to its secrets. The word forbid also means to deny access to a place which in this case is the Pineal gland of sacred knowledge and information.

Kundalini (serpent energy of fire) is defined as follows:

Kundalini, in the concept of Dharma, refers to a form of primal energy said to be located at the base of the spine. Writer Joseph Campbell describes the concept of Kundalini as "the figure of a coiled female serpent—a serpent goddess not of "gross" but "subtle" substance—which is to be thought of as residing in a torpid, slumbering state in a subtle centre, the first of the seven, near the base of the spine: the aim of the yoga then being to rouse this serpent, lift her head, and bring her up a subtle nerve or channel of the spine to the so-called "thousand-petaled lotus" at the crown of the head. She, rising from the lowest to the highest lotus centre will pass through and wake the five between, and with each waking, the psychology and personality of the practitioner will be altogether and fundamentally transformed."

In Egypt the Lotus flower is not only associated with enlightenment but also the balancing of opposites as the twisted branches of the flower intertwine and bind and combine together which was seen as symbolic of combining Upper and Lower Egypt. In other words the priesthoods do not want just anyone knowing this deep and sacred information, the place of knowing, the God-state. The famous tree of the Garden of Eden is the human spine (Bark) and the nervous system, with its filaments and fibre like extensions that acts as the tree's branches. The Garden of Eden is really the human body and Eden means life, it is referring to our physical life as humans, it a physical body/garden in need of nurturing. It was paradise on Earth and a paradise is an ideal or idyllic place or state, namely in this case enlightened consciousness. It has been stated that Eden can be found by the four rivers. Again the four rivers are referring to the fluid systems of the body and those four rivers/fluid systems are:

*Pishon – Urinary system

*Hidikel – Blood

*Gihon – meaning to gush forth and is the intestinal tract

*Euphrates – meaning good water and is the fluid system of the nervous system

Now what about the two main characters of this story Adam and Eve themselves? Adam means man and Eve means life (as does Eden) and Adam is really referring to the 'Organic Atom' and our atomic structure. As I have previously stated, Melanin physics proves that the Black races were the first to inhabit the Earth therefore the depictions given to us by biblical teachings is visually incorrect. When we are told that Eve was created from Adam this is telling us about Ionic bonding which happens when an electron is passed between two atoms. An electron is a current of a negative charge and this is why Eve was seen as a negative influence on the Adam (Atom). Eve is the electron exchange between atoms, the PI- Electron Density in relation to DNA synthesis which is the repair and duplication of cells, which is required in order for them to exist in a chaotic environment within our body. The word body is a Germanic term deriving from Bodig which again means life.

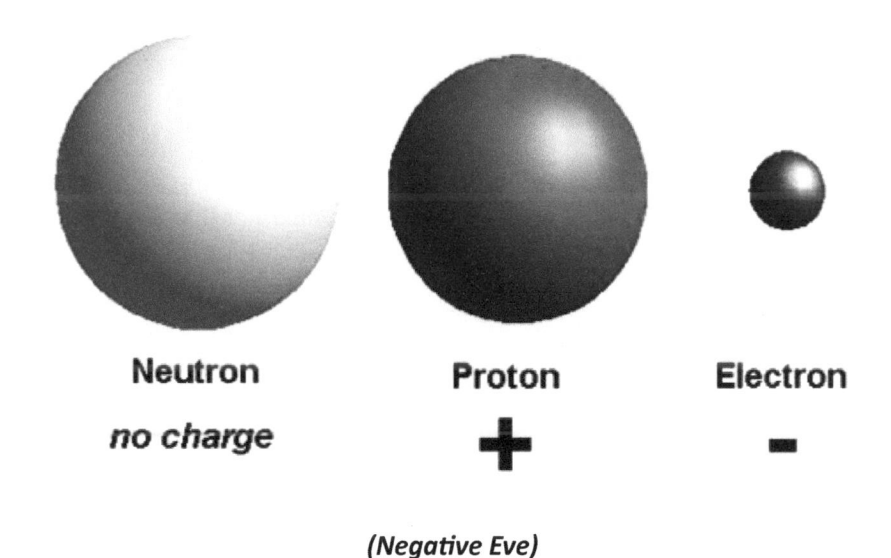

Neutron   **Proton**   **Electron**

no charge   **+**   **−**

(Negative Eve)

The atomic structure also gives rise to the holy trinity, which is the three component parts of the atom, the father is the neutron, the son is the proton and the Holy Ghost is the electron. When electrons become ionised and excited they give off a cloud called an 'electron cloud' and this bears a striking resemblance to a ghost. The Holy Ghost is often also called the Holy Spirit and a spirit is the non-decaying spin of the electron which can enter different realms and dimensions by transiting between magnetic field lines and a magnetic field line is defined as this:

A magnetic field is a force field that is created by moving electric charges and magnetic dipoles, and exerts a force on other nearby moving charges and magnetic dipoles. At any given point, it has a direction and a magnitude, so it is represented by a vector field. The term is used for two distinct but closely related fields denoted by the symbols B and H, where, in the International System of Units, H is measured in units of amperes per meter and B is measured in Tesla's or Newton's per meter per ampere. In a vacuum, B and H are the same aside from units, but in a material with a magnetization, B is solenoidal while H is irrational.

So there you have it, Adam and Eve and the holy trinity are human genetics and the concealment of scared knowledge, the third eye system, the place of knowing, made into a physical story believed by so many people across the whole wide world.

This is the common theme throughout the Bible as you will see as I continue to attribute biblical stories and characters to the genetics of humanity. The powers that be do not want anyone other than the chosen to access the place of sacred knowledge. As a result they have turned it into a place of sin and revenge.

8

Moses: The Mozilla Firefox

Before I move onto the most famous character in the world, namely Jesus, I will firstly go through a few more of the famous biblical characters and the next in line is Moses. Moses is a famous and well renowned character in his own right, he was at odds with the Pharaoh and he was the guide and guardian of the Israelites, Israelites meaning 'Gods chosen Ones' leading them across the desert sands to ultimate safety and residence. But even Israeli archaeologists have now stated that after 70 years of excavation in the area where the so-called exodus (In Greek meaning the road out) took place there has been no evidence found to support this version of the biblical story. So why is that, why has no physical evidence ever been found? If thousands of people had resided in these areas for 40 years then there would be evidence of that, bearing in mind this happened only a couple of thousands of years ago and yet we are finding dinosaur fossils over 65 million years old! Again the simple answer to that is that it is not a physical event, it is a genetic event that happens inside our human body, the universe within, and therefore it cannot be any actual physical evidence in the desert of Sinai and the areas where this exodus was meant to have taken place, because it didn't.

Moses and his people were supposedly in the wilderness for 40 years but in numerology the number 40 represents transition or change, the concept of renewal and a new beginning, with a power to lift the spiritual state. In other words it is the raising of consciousness which you will see as the general theme and hidden meaning of this story, hence the reason that specific number was chosen.

So let us analyse what really happened!

Moses meaning 'Drawn from the water' was found in a basket by a river and was raised by influential adoptive parents according to the biblical account. In adulthood Moses challenged the Pharaoh, performed miracles and parted the red sea whilst the Egyptian army were in pursuit of his people. He created serpents out of thin air and he gave his people the 10 commandments, quite a busy and purposeful life.

So onto Moses, within the human body there is a protective soluble water membrane around our cells called the 'Fluid Mosaic Membrane' and the word Mosaic means Moses. So we can soon see that Moses is part of human genetics and not a physical man, albeit we all have Moses leading the Israelites within us.

Membranes are made of a double layer of lipids, mainly phospholipids, containing embedded proteins. The embedded proteins are important as facilitators in moving molecule through the membrane. The membrane itself is organized into a bimolecular layer meaning that the non-polar region is organized in the middle (away from water as it is hydrophobic – God did not want the Israelites to cross the sea!) and the polar regions are oriented toward the outside: the extracellular fluid and the cytosol. Another way to think of it is two rows of pins with their heads to the outside and the needle part to the inside. Heads, needles,needles, heads Like a sandwich. As the phospholipid molecules are not chemically bound to each other and thus each molecule is free to move independently, the overall bi-layer structure has a flexible fluidity. Cholesterol molecules are also embedded in the plasma membrane and serve to deliver substances to cell organelles by forming vesicles.

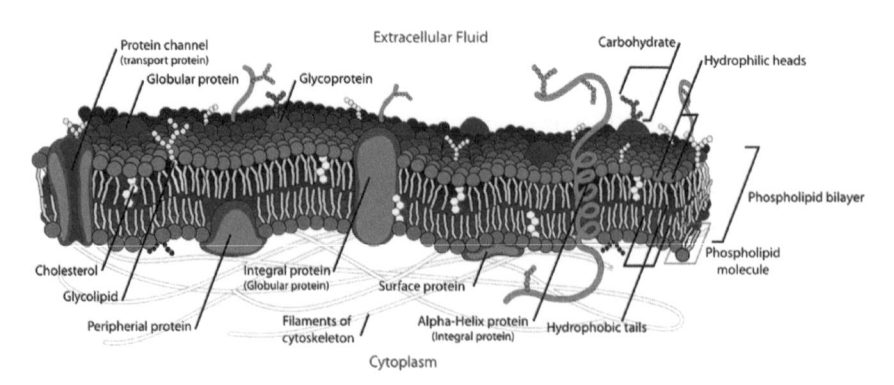

(Cell membrane structure)

Membranes are a protective barrier that stops some things entering and allows others to pass through, which is the story of the people of Moses being allowed to pass the parted waters of the red sea and the Egyptian army not being allowed to pass as the waves came in on them. It is the function of the membrane at work.

The proteins embedded in membrane are categorized into two classes:

Peripheral membrane proteins are proteins on the membrane surface, mainly the cystolic side where they interact with cytoskeletal elements in order to influence cell shape and motility. These proteins are not amphipathic and are bound to Polar Regions of the integral proteins.

Integral membrane proteins span the entire width of the membrane, thus crossing through both the polar and non-polar regions of the structure. These proteins cannot be removed from the membrane without disrupting the lipid bi-layer.

Membranes contain a food vacuole which is called a membrane-enclosed cell vacuole with a digestive function, containing material taken up in by the process of phagocytosis. These are found in amoeba, protozoa, paramecium. In protozoa, whatever the mode of heterotrophic nutrition or diet, the food material is enclosed in food vacuoles, which are bounded by cell membrane and as the biblical story tells us, Moses fed the Israelites, which is really the describing the feeding procedure of the cell membrane. The genetic cells of the human body are the biblical Israelites protected by the Mosaic membrane (Moses). A membrane is a selective barrier and it allows some things to pass through but stops others. Such things may be molecules, ions, or other small particles. Biological membranes include cell membranes, nuclear membranes, which cover a cell nucleus, and tissue membranes, such as mucosae and serosae.

A vacuole is a membrane-bound organelle which is present in all plant and fungal cells and some protist, animal and bacterial cells. Vacuoles are essentially enclosed compartments which are filled with water containing inorganic and organic molecules including enzymes in solution, though in certain cases they may contain solids which have been engulfed. Vacuoles are formed by the fusion of multiple membrane vesicles and are effectively just larger forms of these. The organelle has no basic shape or size, its structure varies according to the needs of the cell. The thylakoid membrane is the site of the light-dependent reactions of photosynthesis with the photosynthetic pigments embedded directly in the membrane. It is an alternating pattern of dark and light bands measuring one nanometre each. Thylakoid membranes are the same family as Mosaic membranes and when the bible tells us that Moses fed the Israelites with Manna bread (Prana) this is the process of human photosynthesis obtained from the sun. Bread is used in many cultures to highlight the relationship between the nourishment of the body and the nourishment of the soul, it is the celestial food which also equates to knowledge. So we have Moses (Fluid Mosaic membrane) feeding the Israelites (cells of the body fed by the food vacuole membranes) with Manna bread (Thylakoid photosynthesis membranes). It is genetic once again!

Photosynthesis is defined as:

"Photosynthesis is a process used by plants and other organisms to convert light energy into chemical energy that can later be released to fuel the organisms' activities. This chemical energy is stored in carbohydrate molecules, such as sugars, which are synthesized from carbon dioxide and water – hence the name photosynthesis, from the Greek φῶς, phōs, "light", and σύνθεσις, synthesis, "putting together".

In most cases, oxygen is also released as a waste product. Most plants, most algae, and cyanobacteria perform photosynthesis, such organisms are called photoautotrophs. Photosynthesis is largely responsible for producing and maintaining the oxygen content of the Earth's atmosphere, and supplies all of the organic compounds and most of the energy necessary for life on Earth. It is all about genetics and our microscopic internal universe.

Now moving onto other parts of the Moses story:

Moses was at odds with the Pharaoh and Egypt was attacked by ten plagues but instead of real events these plagues are happening within the human body.

THE FIRST PLAGUE: WATER CHANGED TO BLOOD

Blood represents regeneration and the fire element of life. Blood is the soul's vehicle or sheath, which is why the life is in the blood. The first plague is in Aries, the House of the Hidden Manna and Manna is Prana (light from the Sun). Misuse of the Creative Fire caused the first plague. Turning water into blood symbolizes the degradation of purity. Egypt needed to return to their original belief in the immortality of the soul.

THE SECOND PLAGUE: FROGS

Frogs belong to the water element. Symbolically they represent the emotional life and human nature. To Egypt it represented the Nile inundation that fertilized their fields. When we enslave the Creative Fire to the outer senses we are infertile. Egypt was being compelled to awaken and free the Creative Fire to become the Flame of God.

THE THIRD PLAGUE: LICE

Lice represent all lesser negative thoughts that upset emotions and bring fear and doubt.

THE FOURTH PLAGUE: SWARMS OF FLIES

Winged insects represent the air element, and they symbolize doubts and thoughts of fear. Wrong thinking created the flies, not emotions.

THE FIFTH PLAGUE: PESTILENCE ON CATTLE

This plague represents the lower animal nature and all overindulgence of self. This plague teaches the balance of inner and outer. It is the bloodstained Path of Spiritual Blindness that results in death in the material world.

THE SIXTH PLAGUE: BOILS

Boils represent hidden emotional frustrations that cause impurities in the bloodstream. The action of boils cleanses the blood and the emotions. Boils represent a physical, bodily revolution, the casting out of impurities, and this affliction was supposed to "boil" out impurities.

THE SEVENTH PLAGUE: HAIL

Thunder, hail and fire represent crystallized imagination, emotions and thinking, in that order. Hail is frozen water and symbolizes emotion crystallized into prejudices and opinions that produce paralysis. Thinking is fire that burns and churns crystallized emotions. The low pole of crystallized imagination creates thundering, destructive pictures. Hail is under Sagittarius, the House of Ascension and Conquering to Ascend. We must heat, melt and absorb all crystallization.

THE EIGHTH PLAGUE: LOCUSTS

Locusts represent the clinging, tenacious hold of the subconscious mind over the soul. An east wind brought the locusts and a west wind took them away. East represents resurrection and west represents ascension.

THE NINTH PLAGUE: DARKNESS FOR THREE DAYS

Three are the number of the master glands in the brain, namely the Pineal, the Pituitary and the Thalamus. Three is the number of perfected personal expression. Three days is the time it takes to cleanse the subconscious mind and ascend to God. Darkness is under the Aquarius Division and the air element. Air (Aquarius is an air sign) represents the Mind of God as us.

THE TENTH PLAGUE: DEATH OF THE FIRST BORN

The tenth Plague is in keeping with theme of genetics within the body there is a mechanism whereby when a cell is dying it notifies other cells so that they can avoid being affected or contaminated. They give off a red dye called 'mito-genetic radiation' or 'mito-reds'. It is the angel, which means messenger, of death! The story of the red dye around the doorframes of the first born is really telling us about this process of genetics. The angel of death sees the mito-reds, a cell in difficulty, and passes by.

The human body is teaming with protons which account for 1/3 of the atomic balance of our cells carried in our blood stream. This blood transit is our cells being bourne (first-born) which means to convey or carry. Proton can also mean proto as in proto-type meaning the first, this is the first-bourne mentioned in the bible.

A proton is defined as this:

"A proton is a subatomic particle, symbol p or p+, with a positive electric charge of +1e elementary charge and mass slightly less than that of a neutron. Protons and neutrons, each with masses of approximately one atomic mass unit, are collectively referred to as "nucleons".

Now what about the crossing of the red sea? The red sea is referring to cerebral blood and its crossing is symbolic in this case of what is known as the 'Cross Translation' of the easy sea, in other words the journey from inner consciousness to outer consciousness, outer consciousness also being higher consciousness. It is the transit made during spiritual awakening which becomes more relevant in just a few moments with the burning bush and Mount Sinai. Inner consciousness is the mind which has many planes of mental activity beyond this is outer consciousness. The crossing of this sea is the transition from inner to outer consciousness maintaining correlation of the two. Again going back to our wonderful genetic world, we have enzymes that open up the double helix strands of DNA and go inside them to repair and fix the damaged or corrupted cells/DNA. Once inside, to prevent any other contaminates following in behind them or even to escape the rectification and cell cleansing process, they close up the double helix strands behind themselves, in effect trapping the contaminates.

This is also the story of the pursuing Egyptian army being trapped by the waves of the parting red sea and subsequent closing of the water that came crashing down on them and their pursuing chariots. It is cell division that describes the parting of the sea. Enzymes are macromolecular biological catalysts. Enzymes accelerate chemical reactions. The molecules upon which enzymes may act are called substrates and the enzyme converts the substrates into different molecules known as products. Almost all metabolic processes in the cell need enzyme catalysis in order to occur at rates fast enough to sustain life. Metabolic pathways depend upon enzymes to catalyse individual steps. The study of enzymes is called enzymology and a new field of pseudo enzyme analysis has recently grown up, recognising that during evolution, some enzymes have lost the ability to carry out biological catalysis, which is often reflected in their amino acid sequences and unusual 'pseudo catalytic' properties.

Moses had a calling and left his people in the desert to scale Mount Sinai and suffered hardship until he eventually reached the summit. It was here that Moses saw the burning bush and spoke to god who gave him the law, the 10 commandments. A mountain is symbolic of a holy place or dwelling of a holy being, god or deity! But the burning bush is really an allegory for the human third eye, the Pineal gland, when activated in spiritual consciousness by the serpent energy of fire, the Kundalini. It is the activation of god-like consciousness. This is the hidden meaning behind the computer logo 'Mozilla Firefox'. Mozilla, as does Mosaic, means Moses and the fox in spiritual animals means spiritual awareness and the fire as previously mentioned is the Kundalini energy of fire awakening this gland. The pineal gland is referred to as the 'face of god' and is also the origin of the biblical story of Jacob fighting the angel on mount penial. Sinai not only means 'Mountain of the Moon' but also means 'Har Bashan' (from the word Beshen) which means with the teeth. The significance of teeth is that they represent exterior intellect natural truth. The teeth also prepare the food for the body which nourishes body and soul. Moses on Mount Sinai is a cryptic message that he was eating celestial knowledge, the food of god, which is a part of the awakening process. The food which nourishes the soul is intelligence and wisdom which is called spiritual and celestial food.

In Matthew 6:22 Jesus stated (and I will reveal the identity of Jesus soon) *"If your eye be single your body will fill with light"* In other words enlightenment will occur through the single eye, the pineal gland and light, bio-photons, are a pinnacle necessity to achieving enlightenment and internal illumination. Bio-photons are photons of light in the ultraviolet and low visible light range that is produced by a biological system. They are non-thermal in origin, and the emission of bio-photons is technically a type of bioluminescence, though bioluminescence is generally reserved for higher luminance. They are used by DNA to send speed of light signals around the body and are the main channel of cellular communication. They are a consciousness connection.

The famous 10 Commandments, commandment meaning to command the mind, is really talking about the brain and the stones are the two hemispheres of the brain. The number 10 is the number of correlation between the spiritual and material realm, the first number of a dual influence from below to above, the connection between inner and outer consciousness. But Moses later smashed the stone tablets and was therefore the first person to 'Break the law'. The fabled 10 commandments that we are taught derived from the 42 negative confessions of Egypt which encompassed the ten categories of sins which are as follows:

1) "General sins against people"
2) "Crimes against a person"
3) "Crimes against the Gods"
4) "Crimes against the King"
5) "Crimes against the Dead"
6) "Crimes against animals"
7) "Crimes against Property"
8) "Fraud"
9) "Faults of morals and character"
10) "Faults of morals and character"

These were then altered to suit the Christian version of history and were developed into the 10 commandments we know of today, namely:

1) I am the Lord thy God. Thou shalt have no other gods before me
2) Thou shalt not make unto thee any graven image...
3) Thou shalt not take the name of the Lord they God in vain
4) Remember the Sabbath day, to keep it holy.
5) Honour thy father and mother
6) Thou shalt not kill.
7) Thou shalt not commit adultery.
8) Thou shalt not steal.
9) Thou shalt not bear false witness against thy neighbour.

10) Thou shalt not covet thy neighbour's house or wife

Not many people realise that by worshipping Jesus they are actually breaking the first commandment.

LIVING IN SIN:

We are told that we are all living in Sin but that really means Sine (sin is an abbreviation of sine) which means the ratio of the side of a right angle. The symbol for 'inverse sine' is sin. Within the body there is what is called the 'transverse plane' that is the one passing horizontally through the body, at right angles to the sagittal and frontal planes and dividing the body into upper and lower portions, heaven and Earth. We are entities of two halves. We were all born with original sin and until our awakening we are living in our lower chakras, the lower part of the transverse plane, the lower density kingdom of Earth (lower chakras) our lower places. We are born in Gods image, The 'Geometry of Divinity' G.O.D. Whereas the Kingdom of heaven is the higher chakras, leading to the God-state which we have not yet reached. Sin/sine in biblical terms is anything that separates us from God, the division of the body into two halves whereby we are living in the lower half is doing just that.

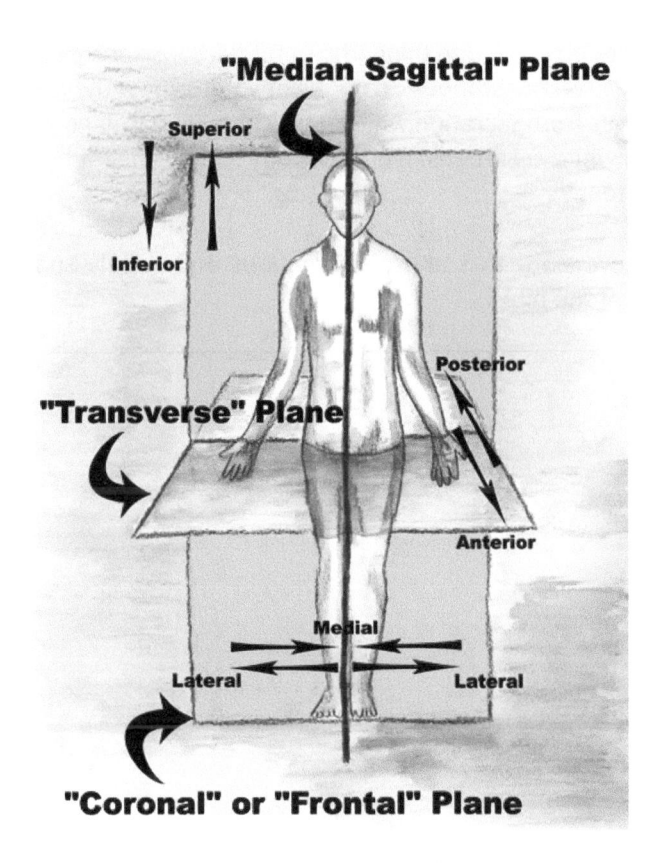

(Transverse Plane)

Jesus was crucified on the cross to save us from sin which takes us from the kingdom of Earth to the kingdom of heaven during the kundalini awakening process, raising us from the lower to the higher places saving us from the lower chakras caused as a result of sine/sin. And as a footnote my nationality is English and English means 'Man of Angles'. When Moses came down from the mountain he saw that his people were carving Bulls and in medical astrology, the connection between the body and the planets, the Bull, Taurus, is the lower mind. Therefore the people were operating from their lower mind and not the Mosaic higher consciousness.

At their deepest levels, this story as with all the other biblical stories I will cite, are all referring to one thing, the potential consciousness awakening of humanity. The priesthoods do not want you to know these secrets and secret derives from secretion which is what the Pineal gland does with its brown and white secretions, which is really what is meant by the land of 'Milk and Honey'.

So let's move onto to some other famous and widely spoken about characters of the bible.

9

Noah: Let Us Now Flood The World With Some Truth

Noah is another world famous historical person from biblical times. According to the bible he was the husband of Emzara and the father of Japheth, Ham, Shem and Yam and his parents were Lamech (father) and Betenos (mother). He was a blameless man who walked faithfully with God. Noah was approached by God and given 120 years warning of an impending disaster and told to build an ark to house all the species of animals and birds on the Earth. Noah was 480 years old when God told him to build an Ark and 600 when it was finished and the vessel itself had a 450 foot beam, was 75 foot in height and had 3 decks. There would have been at least 75,000 animals on board if biblical estimates are correct. But what if, yet again, this is a story to cover up our inner workings within the genetic universe within us all? Well it most certainly is just that. Again we need look no further than the human body to solve the Noah story in order to get a true reflection of what it is really telling us. The Noah story is one of new life that emerges into a new world post flood, but not the great deluge that destroyed life but the human maternal waters of life sustaining protection!

The story of Noah is talking about the wonderful creation of life, the baby in his or her mother's womb. The name Noah means comfort which is exactly what is provided for the unborn child in its mother's womb at the beginning of life. This occurs inside the amniotic sac which provides protection from the outside world until its mother's waters break and the child is ready to emerge into a new world post flood upon the breaking of the maternal waters. The amniotic sac is Noah's ark encasing the child. According to the Talmud, a religious Jewish book, it takes 40 days for an embryo to be formed in its mother's womb and of course the bible tells us that it rained for 40 days and 40 nights. In a spiritual sense this is also referring to the 'Mikveh' which is a bath used for the Jewish rite of purification which must be filled with 40 Se'ahs which is a measure of water. Immersion into the Mikveh is the consummate Jewish symbol of spiritual renewal.

Throughout this book I have and will talk about genetics and our DNA being the building blocks of life, which is a fundamental component part of the ancient code.

DNA, the building blocks of life, exists as and is built upon base pairs, a miracle that some genealogists actually call the '2 by 2 of chromosomes'. This is what the story of the animals went in 2 by 2 actually means at its deepest level of meaning, it is referring to the base pairs of human DNA that exist 2 by 2, namely Adenine and Thymidine and Cytosine and Guanine. (A+T/C+G). A Chromosome is a DNA molecule with part or all of the genetic material of an organism. Most eukaryotic chromosomes include packaging proteins which aided by chaperone proteins, bind to and condenses the DNA molecule to prevent the DNA from becoming an unmanageable tangle. A eukaryote is defined as any organism whose cells have a cell nucleus and other organelles enclosed within membranes. Eukaryotes belong to the domain eukaryota or eukarya, and can be unicellular or multicellular organisms. The defining feature that sets eukaryotic cells apart from prokaryotic cells is that they have membrane-bound organelles, especially the nucleus, which contains the genetic material enclosed by the nuclear membrane. The presence of a nucleus gives eukaryotes their name, which comes from the Greek εὖ and κάρυον. Eukaryotic cells also contain other membrane-bound organelles such as mitochondria and the Golgi apparatus. In addition, plants and algae contain chloroplasts. Unlike unicellular archaea and bacteria, eukaryotes may also be multicellular and include organisms consisting of many kinds of tissue and cell types.

A base pair is a unit consisting of two nucleobases bound to each other by hydrogen bonds. They form the building blocks of the DNA double helix, and contribute to the folded structure of both DNA and RNA. Dictated by specific hydrogen bonding patterns, Watson-Crick base pairs allow the DNA helix to maintain a regular helical structure that is subtly dependent on its nucleotide sequence. The complementary nature of this based-paired structure provides a backup copy of all genetic information encoded within double-stranded DNA. The regular structure and data redundancy provided by the DNA double helix make DNA well suited to the storage of genetic information, while base-pairing between DNA and incoming nucleotides provides the mechanism through which DNA polymerase replicates DNA, and RNA polymerase transcribes DNA into RNA. Many DNA-binding proteins can recognize specific base pairing patterns that identify particular regulatory regions of genes.

The mother's heartbeat, the heart being an electromagnetic generator, is amplified within the amniotic sac which is heard by the baby and offers reassurance and comfort (Noah). It is an electrical circuit of the body that is being concealed with the word ark. When we change the word arc to ark, the 'K' is the lettered symbol of an electrical circuit and relay system. Biphasic (having two phases) electrical currents stimulate promoting both proliferation (rapid reproduction of a cell, part, or organism) and differentiation (development from the one to the many) of fetal neural stem cells.

The whole story of Noah and the ark is telling us about the wonderment that is the creation and home of the new foetus and how it emerges into a new world post flood. It is not really talking about a wooden boat and a multitude of global animal species.

We truly need to start looking into the depths of these so called flood waters in order to locate and discover the true meanings that are hidden below the water's surface tension and we must stop stopping before we dip our heads below the water line. Because the truth is hidden there!

10

Mary And Joseph:
The Water And The Seed

Mary And Joseph: The Water And The Seed

The land of Judea, part of modern Israel, was ruled by King Herod meaning 'song of the hero'. This land was Nazareth meaning Priest-Kings, but it didn't actually exist by this name in biblical times, despite biblical claims. Two residents lived in this land during these times and they were Mary, deriving from Mare meaning water and Joseph meaning 'God will add the seed' which is quite relevant in the next chapter.

They were engaged but not yet married. Then one evening Mary lay in bed in what was to be a night with a difference. During the stillness and darkness of the night Mary was awoken by the archangel Gabriel. The archangel told Mary to not be afraid and that she would be the mother of the son of God, which is a strange event and not the usual type of night. Joseph was dismayed that a child was to be born out of wedlock and wanted to cancel the wedding but he too was visited by the archangel Gabriel who explained that Mary had been chosen by God to born his child. After the virgin pregnancy Mary and Joseph travelled the 70 miles from Nazareth to the family home of Joseph in Bethlehem. But the only place that they could find to stay in was a barn containing animals and a manger was made out of hay to wrap the forthcoming son of God. The archangel Gabriel announced that on this day the saviour had been born and lay in a manger.

When Jesus was born a new star appeared in the sky and this then lead the three wise men to follow seeking the son of God as news of his arrival spread fast throughout the land. The star had navigated the three wise men, the magi (magicians) to the birth place of Jesus.

So what is the real story?

Well there are two versions, one of them is astronomy which I will reveal first and then there is the genetic version of the story which I will reveal second.

In astronomy the three wise men are the three stars of the belt of the constellation of Orion, namely Alnitak, Alnilam and Mintaka and the star they are evidently following in the sky is Sirius 'A' which is the fabled star of Bethlehem!

(The three wise men and the star of Bethlehem)

In Egypt the star of Bethlehem was a flower used to stimulate the three components parts of the third eye system the process of which is called the 'Bach remedy'.

Sirius 'A' (known as the cosmic egg) is also associated with the Egyptian goddess of motherhood Isis, from whom mother Mary is the Christianised version. In the same region of sky there is the constellation of Cancer which contains a cluster of stars called the 'manger' and two stars called Asellus Borealis and Asellus Australis which in Latin means North Donkey and South Donkey. This is the Donkey used to convey the pregnant Mary to Bethlehem. Jesus was born between the Goat and the horse which is the constellations of Capricorn and Sagittarius. Mother also belongs to the same family of words as matter, material and mater meaning the physical world. The gold, frankincense, and myrrh bought as gifts by the three wise men is representing and is symbolic of the three component parts of the human third eye and consciousness which I go into more detail about in the next chapter which explains the identity of Jesus himself!

So now I have explained the astronomical significance let me explain the genetic version of Mary and Joseph. Mary and Joseph were depicted sitting either side of Jesus at either side of the manger. In bodily terms Mary and Joseph are the Ida and Pingala nerves, which are the two energy channels for the flow of feminine (Moon) and Masculine (Sun) energies. And when the two opposites become balanced they wake up kundalini energy, the divine serpent energy (the serpent fire) within. The kundalini then begins its ascent up the shushumna nadi which is situated between the Ida and Pingala nerves which stem from the brain, the Ida from the Pituitary gland and the Pingala from the Pineal gland. The Pituitary gland deals with lactation and motherhood, hence the term 'Mother Mary'. As kundalini energy ascends it provokes the birth of the divine Christ consciousness, the Christ seed, the saviour which means 'He who sows the seed' but again this will be delved into in the next chapter where I will discuss the genetic life of Jesus and also reveal the identity of his potential wife Mary Magdalene. The Ida nerve is known as the lunar nerve that acts as a coolant, it is the moon controlled water and Mary means water. The Ida and Pingala converge through the 'semi-lunar ganglion', the cranial nerves, which has Christ connections, but also act as the 12 tribes of Israel laying siege upon the biblical walls of Jerico which are the bony structure of the human skull. Jerico means 'city of the Moon' so named because of the semi-lunar ganglion, semi-lunar means crescent Moon and ganglion is a nerve network. So the nativity play acted out by millions of children worldwide every year without fail, the story of Mary and Joseph and as you will soon understand the birth of the Christ, belongs to both the sky and inner universe of the unseen genetic world, the connection being housed by 'medical astrology'.

Medical astrology (traditionally known as Iatromathematics which is an astrological diagnosis, this is the use of astrology to aid the diagnosis and treatment of illness) is an ancient medical system that associates various parts of the body, diseases, and drugs as under the influence of the sun, moon, and planets, along with the twelve astrological signs.

And now in the next chapter the 'Greatest story ever told', will be finally correctly told!

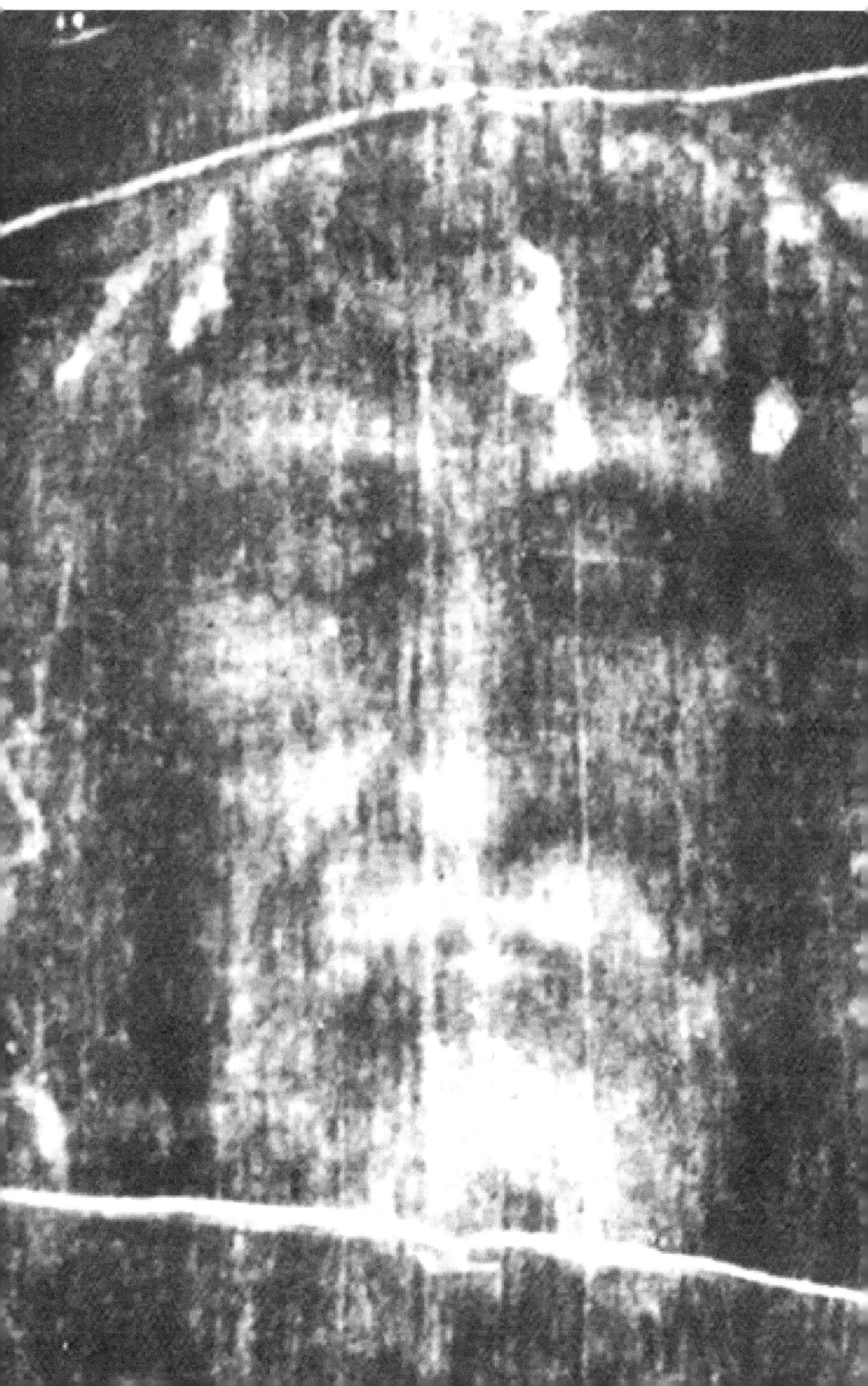

11

Jesus: What Is The Truth For Christ Sake?

So the son of God was born of Mary in a stable wrapped in hay. He was to become the most famous man to have ever supposedly lived on planet Earth, the mere utterance of opposition provokes the screams of blasphemy and heresy (which means to choose), even over two thousand years later. So Jesus (whose name derives from 'Ieous' meaning 'Son of Zeus, which is the planet Jupiter), began his father's work in the Temples aged just 12 and was baptised aged 30. He was born in the age of Pisces which is the age of deception, which is extremely relevant. Mary and Joseph became worried that Jesus had disappeared but upon seeing them Jesus said *"Why did you have to look for me"? 'Didn't you know that I had to be in the house of my Father"?* Temple means House of God and it is really inside the human head where Jesus is both crucified and resurrected which I will now detail.

We do of course have two Jesus's, the Earthly Jesus and the resurrected and ascended heavenly Jesus, both of which I will reveal in this chapter and the next starting with the Earthly Christ. In a world of fertility cults and a Roman empire, who embarked in mass orgies to create sexual energy, that also had a major influence in the direction of Christianity under Emperor Constanine, it makes perfect sense for the story to contain a fertility code. But Jesus the man did not exist, he is an allegory and this has been confirmed both historically by Pope Leo X who stated that *"It has served us well this myth of Christ"* and more recently the current Pope Francis who stated that *"Jesus is metaphorical, not literal"*, at a Catholic Mass at the end of 2017. Fertility even stems to Hinduism with their festival of light, Diwali which is symbolic of seeds of light (fireworks) impregnating the cosmic womb (sky). Do people realise that by worshipping the figure Jesus they are breaking the first commandment?

EARTHLY CHRIST:

At puberty, around the biblically apt age of 12 in males, (Jesus begins his father's work aged 12) we develop what is known as the solar seed or Christ seed which is a phenomenon that occurs in the testicles which are themselves connected to the solar plexus by a network of nerves called the Celiac plexus. Celiac means belly and plexus is a nerve network. This is more commonly known as male sperm and the word sperm means seed.

In fact the title given to Jesus namely the 'Saviour' in itself means 'He who sows the seed'. Male sperm is the Christ seed/solar seed which is the real virgin birth of the Earthly Jesus Christ, Jesus is male sperm and sperm becomes 'anointed', the title given to Jesus, by semen. Anointed means to oil or become oiled. The Christ seed is the Christos seed and Christos means to anoint which means to oil. It becomes the anointed one.

The solar plexus is known as 'Bethlehem' which means 'House of bread'. Therefore we have Jesus born in Bethlehem. To be even more detailed, within the solar plexus there is a thimble sized depression called both the 'Manger' and the 'Fish'. Therefore Jesus (Christian symbol the fish) was born in a manger in Bethlehem with Mary and Joseph either side of the manger which I mentioned in the previous chapter as being the Ida and Pingala nerves. Jesus was baptised aged 30 by John the Baptist in the river Jordan and Jordan means to flow down or descend. The river Jordan is really the spinal fluids of the human body. The spinal fluids and other fluids of the body contain salt, namely Sodium Chloride and this is our Salvation, Sal meaning Salt. The name Yeshua, also identified with Jesus, means Salvation. In others words we are our own salvation by virtue of our own bodily salts, which convey our Christ seed to our own individual Christ Consciousness. The life of Christ is the workings of the journey of the Christ seed on its way to an enlightened state (Christ Consciousness) and is as follows.

Within the body we have a dormant serpent energy called the Kundalini which actually means 'Coiled serpent' and this lays dormant at the base of the human spine (Jacob's ladder). When activated and awakened it rises up Jacobs ladder (spine) activating the human chakra system and in doing so it travels up Jacobs ladder (snakes and ladders game played as children). Chakras are any centre of the subtle body believed to be a psychic-energy centre in the esoteric traditions of Indian religions. The concept is found particularly in the tantric traditions of Hinduism, Buddhism and Jainism. They are conceived as an energy focal point, bodily functions or psychic node in the subtle body. The Chakra theories are an elaborate part of the Kundalini system. It is simply an energy wheel or an energetic seat within the body. The Kundalini is the serpent fire energy and as it initially moves through the lower chakras, the Earthly chakras of low desire, it burns them with its fire energy. The two lowest chakras are called Sodom and Gomorrah, which in the bible were destroyed by fire, this is what the story of Sodom and Gomorrah is really describing.

The Christ seed is conveyed through the body and ends up in the skull, Golgotha which means 'Place of skulls', having first passed through the crossing (cross) which is the chamber of light or 'Optic Chiasm' within the brain so named by the Greeks, as it resembles a cross, where it is crucified. The word crucified has several meanings and is not the one used in the bible. Crucified also means to subdue ones appetite and this is relevant with what is called 'Sexual Sublimation' or as it is otherwise known 'celibacy' in other words saving the seed and not wasting it. The body refines a tenth of this sexual energy which is where we get the saying 'Tithing' meaning a tenth. Higher consciousness and sexual sublimation, which is diverting sexual energy to the brain, is used for kundalini awakening. Any semen not ejaculated is simply absorbed by the body to be reused by other cells. In females they have a substitute germ called the 'lunar seed'. The lunar germ/seed originates in the pituitary body within the brain and follows a path by way of the fourth ventricle down the spine and into the reproductive organs which combines chemically to aid the production of sperm. If the lunar germ is not lost in sexual activities it travels back into the brain where it combines with the solar germ/solar seed. In each month, after puberty, the generative system produces one of these lunar germs in the pituitary body.

Upon the Christ seeds crucifixion it then goes into the Cerebellum within the brain for the equivalent of one Moon cycle which is 3 days. 3 days is also the time it takes to cleanse the sub-conscious mind and ascend to God. The Christ or more aptly the Christ seed is therefore dead for 3 days in the tomb. At that point the Seed is resurrected which simply means to 'use again' which is exactly what the body does with the refined and unused sexual energy and the seed goes through the third eye system and into cosmic consciousness, the 'Christ Consciousness' symbolised by the crown of thorns which indicates the end of Earthly consciousness before the ascension into higher consciousness, the story of Christ's spiritual journey is describing the kundalini awakening process of enlightened consciousness. It is the 'Rapture of Christ and it is the second coming of the Christ.

Rapture simply means the feeling of ecstasy or the transition from one place to another so in genetic bodily terms this is describing making the journey from the unconscious to the conscious state within ourselves, in other words the awakening or resurrection of our own Christ state.

The first coming is the birth of this inner Christ as described above but the second coming is the journey into this Christ consciousness where we escape the material and physical realm and connect to the ether, the fifth element, which is also relevant on the cross of Christ with the letters INRI above Jesus himself. We are to balance our beings so that we can rule the 4 elements (INRI in Latin are the 4 elements) and reach the 5th element, our God-state. INRI stands for:

IAM

NOUR

RUACH

IABESHA

In the biblical scripture John 14:6 Jesus stated that *"I am the way and the truth and the life. No one comes to the Father except through me"*. The Thalamus within the brain and part of the third eye system is known as the gateway or 'RU' so in other words no one can reach the cosmic consciousness awakening without going 'through/thRU' the third eye system, the gateway to a higher place! It is also what is being referred to in the numerous biblical witnessed visitations of the 'Chariots'. In old Hebrew the Merkaba is called the Chariot and it is the vessel in which to travel to and reach higher consciousness. The night before the crucifixion Jesus and the 12 disciples gathered for a last supper also known as the Lord's supper. So what is this telling us?

The 12 Earthly Disciples of Christ are the 12 cranial nerves of the brain, namely:

1) Olfactory nerve.

2) Optic Nerve

3) Oculomoter nerve

4) Trochlear nerve

5) Trigeminal nerve

6) Abducens nerve

7) Facial nerve

8) Vestibulocochlear nerve

9) Glossopharyngeal nerve

10) Vagus nerve

11) Accessory nerve

12.) Hypoglossal nerve

Jesus sits at the table of the mind, the Mensa. Mensa has a double meaning of both Mind and table and was used during the Lord's Supper (Lord means Giver of Bread) where he says the Lords' prayer, the bread givers great mind, nourished by celestial food of body and soul, knowledge.

"Give us this day our daily bread" in other words give us the seed in which to activate our Christ consciousness so that it may be the same on Earth as it is in heaven, forever and ever 'Amen' (deriving from Amun which means hidden) and this knowledge certainly is hidden. The Lord's prayer is the great mind on Earth (prayer = Praayer) and the conversation between inner consciousness (brain) and outer consciousness (higher consciousness, the father/God-mind). The hand position of a prayer is the balancing of the hand chakras leading to Christ consciousness. Christ consciousness means and indicates a level of consciousness and was never referring to a singular person, a Christ, it has a much broader

meaning relating to all of us and our potential awakening.

Your hands can also tell you about the state of balance of your right side and left side energies. The subtle energy channel on your right side carries your physically and mentally active, outgoing energies, and the channel on your left side, your emotional and passive, receptive energies, "Sun" and "Moon" energies respectively. Your Kundalini rises most strongly when these two energies are in balance. Your fingers and parts of your hands are your sensors of the chakras, each finger corresponds to a chakra (In the lower chakra system). Each chakra has a left and right side. The right side is the male aspect of the chakra, and the left side, the female aspect. Your right hand finger corresponds to the right side of the chakra, and your left hand finger, to the left side.

The fingers that correspond to the chakras are:-

Little finger=Heart chakra.

Ring finger=Third Eye chakra.

Middle finger = Solar Plexus chakra.

First finger = Throat chakra.

Thumb = Sacral / Sexual chakra.

Heel of Palm – Wrist junction = Root chakra.

Centre of Palm = Crown chakra

The concept of wedding rings originated in ancient Egypt and our ring finger is our third eye chakra finger. The gold ring on this finger to me represents consciousness fusion through the balance and union of opposites namely man and women, masculine and feminine.

(Prayer Position)

After the Kundalini has penetrated the Crown chakra, and you have become an enlightened or realised Soul, you also become vibrationally aware, your Kundalini connects to the Kundalini of everyone, everywhere. The last supper or the Lord's Supper is really referring to the soup of the mind. The word supper derives from soup and soup means to enhance the performance or power of, which is really referring to Christ consciousness awakening enhanced by certain practices.

When Jesus says *"Eat My Body, Drink My Blood"* what does it really mean? The Blood aspect means the spiritual union of mind and matter, the Christ consciousness connecting to the father energy, the ether, and *"In Remembrance of me"* which is the death of the old you for a new resurrected consciousness, the old testament to the new testament, testament meaning body and mind. The resurrection of Christ was witnessed by Mary Magdalene, but who was she? Mary Magdalene, the wife of Christ to some, a prostitute to others and the linear blood line of

Christ according to author Dan Brown and his books. But who was this mysterious character?

Magdalene the story - Mainstream version:

"When Christ preached in the country she came – by God's providence – into the house of Simon the leper for she had heard that Christ was going to eat there. Not daring to sit among the just because she was a sinner she walked straight up to the Lord, washed his feet with her tears, dried them with her hair and anointed them, for it was the custom that the people used ointments for the heat of the sun was great. Simon the Pharisee thought "If this were a prophet he would scarcely allow himself to be touched by a sinner." But the Lord punished him because of the superficiality of his justice and forgave the woman for all her sins. This is the Mary Magdalene upon whom God bestowed such great grace and to whom he made evident so many signs of love. He expelled seven evil spirits from her and inspired in her the love for Him. He made her a special friend, a great hostess and a help on His road. He excused her at all times with great love, defended her against the Pharisee who had called her impure, against her sister who had accused her of idleness, and against Judas who had called her a spendthrift. And whenever he saw her weeping he wept, too". (End of mainstream narrative).

I have researched the workings of the human body extensively and I have been able to attribute the biblical characters and stories to such workings of its genetics. As with all the characters I have researched Mary Magdalene is no different. Magdalene in Hebrew means tower and she was known as the 'Tower of Fishermen'. So who was she? Within the brain we have the 3 Mary's namely the Virgin Mary, Mary of Bethany and of course Mary Magdalene. Mary of Magdala is really the Amygdala within the human brain which is so positioned that it witnesses the Crucifixion of the Christ and also his leaving of the tomb which is referring to the Cerebellum.

The Amygdala is the one of the four basal ganglia in each cerebral hemisphere that is part of the limbic system and consists of an almond-shaped mass of grey matter in the anterior extremity of the temporal lobe, called also amygdaloid nucleus. The amygdala is responsible for the perception of emotions such as anger, fear, and sadness, as well as the controlling of aggression. The amygdala helps to store memories of events and emotions so that an individual may be able to recognize similar events in the future. For example, if you have ever suffered a dog bite, then the amygdalae may help in processing that event and, therefore, increase your fear or alertness around dogs. The size of the amygdala is positively correlated with increased aggression and physical behaviour. The amygdala in humans also plays a role in sexual activity and libido, or sex drive, a person's overall sexual drive or desire for sexual activity hence why Mary Magdalene was in some circles known as the Prostitute. It is the female counterpart of the divine masculine, the Christ! (The Wife of Christ)

So Mary Magdalene is part of our brain and compliments our own Christ! Another Mary of the bible was Mary of Bethany whom Jesus asked to relay a message to Mary Magdalene. Beth means house and is synonymous (having the same meaning as another word or phrase in the same language) with the mind. Mary of Bethany is the smaller amygdala of the brain. The smaller amygdala is also involved in emotional processes and alike in line with the larger amygdala (Magdalane) and they work together.

The whole biblical story of the life of Jesus and his subsequent crucifixion and resurrection is really talking about the odyssey of the Christ seed from birth to Christ consciousness awakening and not a real physical story. Jesus is the 'Good Shepherd' also called a 'Feeder' and a good shepherd supplies all that is needed for his flock. Anatomically our solar plexus (house of bread) feeds our brain supplying some of its needs. There is a relationship that our solar plexus (abdominal brain) and the brain within our head have together. Therefore, the Lord (giver of bread) is our shepherd, as the place where the Christ seed grows, feeds the brain and our needs.

Jesus turned water into wine as part of the miracles of Christ which is really the ingested water of the body being transmuted into our bloodstream and being used as part of our bodily functions. Red wine is symbolic of blood as we see in the likes of Holy Communion celebrations. Jesus tells us all this in Colossians 1:17 "And he is before all things and in and through him the universe is a harmonious whole and in him all things are held together. This is again really talking of the inner workings of the body. Within the body we have a cross shaped glue called Laminin which holds muscles and tissues and internal bodily fibres together.

(Cross shaped Laminin)

Laminins are high-molecular weight proteins of the extracellular matrix. They are a major component of the basal lamina, a protein network foundation for most cells and organs. The laminins are an important and biologically active part of the basal lamina, influencing cell differentiation, migration, and adhesion. They are also used in the bodies defence against illness which is why Jesus heals the sick! The abbreviation of the Laminin is LAMB3 (3 = component parts of the atom) this is the L.A.M.B of God, Jesus (Lamb of God).

Jesus ironically dies aged 33 which is the hertz frequency of Christ Consciousness and again this is no coincidence and not a randomly chosen irrelevant number, it has been chosen specifically due to its hidden code. The Earthly Christ has ascended and goes back to the heavens (sky). The birth of the Christ seed is the beginning of the Christ consciousness process and the crucifixion is the end which is why Jesus biblically states in Revelation 22:13 "I am the Alpha and the Omega, the First and the Last, the Beginning and the End".

The five wounds of Christ symbolise the pentagram, the number 5, which is the number of 'realised man' and the inner dimensions of the pentagram are 108 degrees. 108 in terms of hertz is the frequency of 'all knowing. This aspect of the story is also telling us about our own consciousness.

And when the bible talks of the many chariots seen in the sky that is a metaphor for the merkaba which is the vehicle that takes us to higher consciousness. In old Hebrew the word merkaba means chariot.

When we know the true esoteric meanings of these works of concealed genius we take part in our own personal Jonah and the whale story. The whole story of Jonah and the whale is one of leaving spiritual darkness (belly of the whale) and emerging into spiritual light (leaving the belly of the whale) which is what the story of Jonah and the whale is really telling us. The whale or leviathan was an ancient symbol of spiritual darkness. It is our 'Epiphany' deriving from the word epiphysis meaning Pineal gland. And as Jesus stated in the biblical scriptures in Mathew 6:22 *"If your eye be single, your whole body shall be full of light"*. This is secretly telling us about our Pineal gland and enlightenment (Pineal gland is our single eye). There has been several invented finds such as the shroud of Turin that some say is the imprint of the body of Christ which is really wishful thinking and deceptive delusion on their part. Especially when you have people such as Brian Leonard Golightly Marshall who claims to be Jesus returned and the actual imprint on the shroud of Turin, others also claim to be modern day Jesus returned. Brian Leonard Golightly Marshall was the subject of the Monty Python satire film called 'Life of Brian' (could also have been called 'Life of Brain').

Christ the physical man as biblically described did not exist. We are given this information when we actually take the time to examine what is said in the biblical scriptures, but not many people do, for example in Luke 17:21 which gives a Jesus quotation and says:

"The Kingdom of God is not something people will be able to see and point to for behold the Kingdom of God is within you". Exactly, Jesus and the Kingdom of God within us is human genetics as pointed out throughout this book and in this chapter!

So now I have identified the real Earthly Christ what happens to him after his ascension back to the father?

You are about to find out in the next chapter.

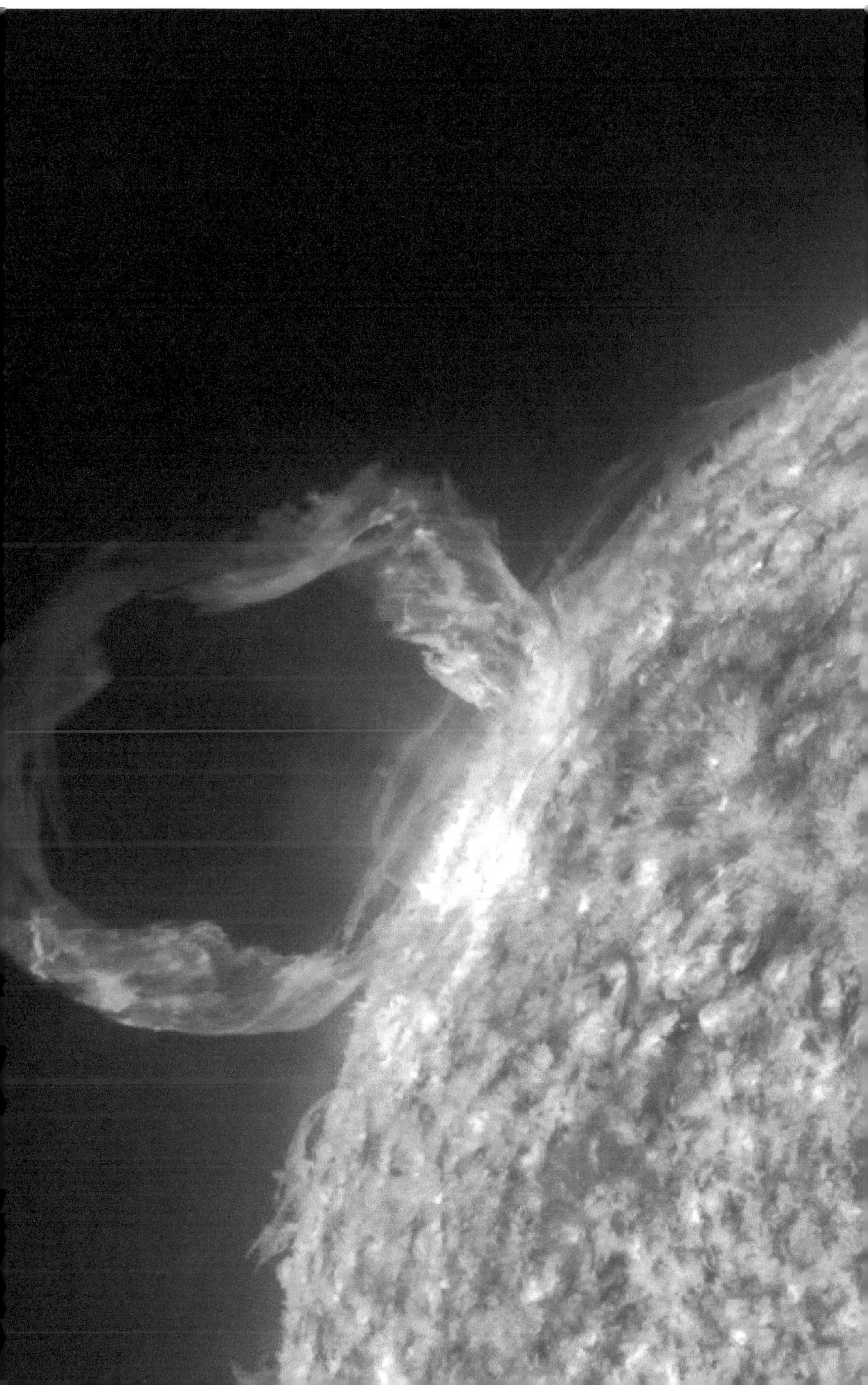

12

The Ascended Christ: Post Crucifixion – Back In The Heavens

Imagine ancient man looking up at the sky and seeing an array of bright luminous dots scattered everywhere, no street lighting to block his view of these stars which mapped out the sky and gave him an idea of the time of the calendar year by virtue of star movement. An indicator of light that never changed and could be relied upon as an accurate measure of which he became a 'master', which means 'Measurer of stars'. The world religions are at their origins really astrotheology which is the worship of stars and other heavenly bodies as deities, or the association of deities with heavenly bodies. The most common instances of this are sun gods and moon gods in polytheistic systems worldwide. Also notable is the association of the planets with deities in Babylonian. In the most prominent world Religions they worship unknowingly the 7 visible planets of our solar system namely, Mercury, Venus, Mars, Jupiter, Saturn, Moon and the Sun.

The heavenly Jesus is the solar Sun, which is the foundation of Christianity and Christianity is nothing more or nothing less than Sun worship carried out at Sun-day service! Jesus has reached sainthood along with his heavenly disciples. Sainthood or a saint is simply someone who is of sufficient sanctity to take their place in heaven and the word heaven in many languages means sky. In other words Jesus has now reached the sky. In astronomy Mother Mary is Sirius 'A' and Joseph is Orion, both of these stars are different characters in Egypt and I will get onto that later in the ancient Egyptian chapter. Just ask yourself this question, if the creator of all things is a mathematician that has brought into being a system of duplication and replication why would he have only one 'begotten' sun? The Sun, Jesus, in the bible was crucified between the two biblical thieves which are really the two solstices, (solstice means Sun standing still), the good thief and the bad thief so called because one takes the sun (winter – bad thief takes the sun) and the good thief (summer – good thief gives the Sun), set below the Southern Cross, the 4 star constellation.

On 22nd, 23rd and 24th December each year the sun remains in the same degree of sky and is dead for 3 days. Then on 25th December each year the sun moves 1 degree north to continue its annual transit of the zodiac, the sun is therefore born on 25th December, which may be a familiar date, that being the festival of Christ at Christmas. The bible tells us that

Jesus rose early on the first day of the week, which is Sunday at sunrise, the resurrection of the Son/Sun.

Even the feeding of the 5000 with 5 loaves and 2 fishes has astronomical connotations. Virgo, the house of bread, the 5th house of the zodiac, is the zodiac opposite of Pisces, the two fishes and here we have the biblical 5 loaves and 2 fish's story encrypted within the stars. The planets and the zodiac are the heavenly key to the answer to the resurrected Jesus now that he has ascended beyond the Earthly Christ. Even the miracle of walking on water is the solar Sun's reflection upon the water itself.

(Jesus walking on water)

And when we see the spectacular crimson sky of either sunset or sunrise this is the 'Blood of Christ'.

The term astro-theology is used in the context of 18th to 19th century scholarship aiming at the discovery of the original religion, particularly primitive monotheism. Unlike astrolatry, which usually implies polytheism, frowned upon as idolatrous (relating to or practising idolatry, idol-worshipping) by Christian authors since Eusebius, astrotheology is any "religious system founded upon the observation of the heavens" and in particular, may be monotheistic.

Babylonian astronomy from early times associates stars with deities, but the heavens as the residence of an anthropomorphic (having human characteristics) pantheon, and later of monotheistic God and his retinue of angels, is a later development, gradually replacing the notion of the pantheon residing or convening on the summit of high mountains. Depending upon which major religion you follow depends upon which planet or planets are prominent within your belief systems.

Islam is mainly Moon and Venus worship with a pinch of Saturn. Allah means 'the Moon' in the Egyptian Afro-asiatic language. Allah is a later version of Hubal who was the Moon God worshipped in Kaaba (in Mecca meaning cube) and there we have the Kaaba-Allah which leads onto Judaism and the Kabballah! Hubal's symbol was the crescent Moon which without coincidence is upon every Mosque. Islam is basically pagan Moon worship. Muslims plan their year by a Lunar calendar called the Hijri and have their religious fasting during the night, the domain of the Moon and in the morning they break their fast (Breakfast). The Sun and Moon are opposites, therefore so are Islam and Christianity, Christianity being Sun worship and Islam being Moon worship. They are the two great luminaries of the sky. Even the promise of 72 virgins to the martyrs of terrorism is really pagan astronomy.

(Pentacle)

The points of the pentagram touch the circle of the pentacle every 72 degrees and Venus in zodiac astrological terms is the sub-ruler of Virgo which in Latin means virgin. Venus is symbolised as the pentagram as it has a pentagram shaped orbit. Add these component parts together we get the 72 virgins, a fake promise hardly worth dying for. And since this, like any other religion, is male dominated they don't want women to have a divine connection so symbolically it is severed with the likes of the Hijab which means barrier or partition.

Both Judaism and Islam revere the 'Black box' which is a little leather box that Orthodox Jews tie around their heads in some solemn moments which is called the tefillin and is a very old Jewish tradition. The tefillin contain scriptures from the Torah folded up in the little box as a symbolism that the Jews will always remember the scriptures. In Islam the Black Stone of Mecca, or Kaaba Stone, is a Muslim relic, which according to Islamic tradition dates back to the time of Adam and Eve. It is the eastern cornerstone of the Kaaba, the ancient sacred stone building towards which Muslims pray, in the centre of the Grand Mosque in Mecca, Saudi Arabia.

Catholicism is another one of the world's most popular belief systems and Catholic means universal and it worships the 7 visible planets in various combinations. So Judaism and many of the Semitic religions follow mainly Saturn and Christianity is largely Sun worship. But the faithful followers don't know this.

So what about the heavenly Christ? When Jesus was crucified and resurrected as stated in the previous chapter we are told that he returned to the heavens (sky) to be with his father. The father of the sky is the planet Jupiter in astrological terms. The name Jesus derives from Ieous which means 'Son of Zeus' (Zeus is the planet Jupiter). The symbol of Zeus is the lightning strike because Jupiter suffers with violent storms. In Hebrew the Sun is called Shamash which means 'servant' and Jesus is the servant of God. As stated in the bible in John 8:12 *"When Jesus spoke again to the people, he said, "I am the light of the world. Whoever follows me will never walk in darkness, but will have the light of life."* Yes, the light of the world is the Sun and when he states that he is also the

'Breath of life' in astronomy this is Prana breathing. Prana or Prāṇāyāma is a Sanskrit word alternatively translated as "extension of the prāṇa "or "breath control." Oxygen is the Earthly breath of life and Prana is the heavenly breath of life. The word is composed from two Sanskrit words: prana meaning life force, and either ayama or the negative form ayāma, meaning to extend or draw out. It is a yogic discipline with origins in ancient India. It is basically a human photosynthesis known as 'Mana' in the Polynesian language. Jesus also states that he is the bread of life and Mana bread is supposedly what Moses fed the Israelites during the exodus! This is of course the celestial food of knowledge rather than physical bread.

So Jesus is the Solar sun surrounded by his 12 heavenly disciples (Disciples = Disc = Zodiac wheel) which are the 12 signs of the Zodiac, the wheel of Gad (will of God). The personalities of the disciples stated in the bible are really the traits of their zodiac signs and anyone who has ever experienced an astrology reading such as a natal chart will know that the stars and planets have a large influence and impact on us and form our characteristics. A natal chart is an astrological chart cast on the basis of when and where an individual was born, also, a horoscope based on this, also called [natal horoscope] Examples. A natal chart is calculated for the time, date, and geographical location of a specific person.

These are the 12 disciples and their corresponding zodiac sign, (they are also the 12 tribes of Israel):

* Aries: Peter, the fiery, impulsive, changeable, pioneering leader

*Taurus: Simon Zelotes, the dogmatic, determined zealot, who was concerned with property and finances, rebelled against the payment of taxes

* Gemini: James, "the lesser." Slow to accept the authenticity of the Messiah

* Cancer: Andrew, the sympathetic homebody

* Leo: John, the most beloved apostle

* Virgo: Philip, always precise, calculating, enquiring, and practical

* Libra: Bartholomew-Nathaniel, the innocently pure one, the tactful evangelist

* Scorpio: Thomas, the doubting sceptic, yet bold and courageous

* Sagittarius: James, the great teacher

* Capricorn: Matthew, the tax gatherer, the politician

* Aquarius: Thaddeus-Jude, who considered the lot of the peasant, and sought to better the living and working conditions of the masses

* Pisces: Judas Iscariot, who when he succumbed to temptation suffered severe pangs of remorse

So without the Sun there is no life on Earth, we owe it a debt of gratitude. It is no surprise then in that case that many brotherhoods around the world succumb to a form of Sun worship. Every day we all see at least 1000 numerous symbols. They derive from this planetary body that we often just pass by without a second thought or any knowledge of its origin such as the fast food chain McDonalds. McDonalds: The golden arches are the gateway of the temple of Solomon and the word Solomon is the sun in three languages. Sol (Latin) Om (Hindu) and On (Coptic Egyptian). The Hindu's believed that the sound OM was the primordial sound that created the universe and its frequency wavelength is 7.23cm, incidentally which is the same distance between the chakras of the human body. The McDonalds symbol on its side reads the number 13 which is the number of heavenly government, Jesus plus the 12 disciples = 13. The examples are really endless and extremely widespread even amongst company logos and brand names such as Nissan (meaning April) whose logo is the Passover (sun passing over the equator) or the time of Easter amongst Christians who needed an alternative name for this period of Sun activity than the one created by Judaism.

It even goes into the world of confectionary, which is a surprise to most people. So out of all of the examples that I could have chosen I choose a biscuit called 'Oreo' which is a popular brand having sold over 500 million units. Oreo derives from 2 words, namely OR meaning Gold/Golden and EO which comes from the Greek word Eos meaning Dawn. Therefore we have the Golden Dawn, the Sun! If you look closely at the pattern upon the biscuit you will see the 'Double Cross' which is the 'Cross of Lorraine' a heraldic Patriarchal cross. There are also exactly 12 Templar Cross Pattees in a circle, with also 12 dots and 12 dashes. A cross pattée (or "cross patty" or "cross Pate", known also as "cross formée/formy" or croix pattée) is a type of Christian cross. This cross was used by the 'Knights Templars' as their cross of the 'Crusades' which was allowed by the authorities within Jerusalem and was the Christian Cross. The Knights Templar's are today's Illuminati, the 'Enlightened Ones'. So next time you eat an Oreo have a look at its Templar symbology! Even pancake day. The pancake is symbolic of the Solar-Sun and Shrove as in shrove Tuesday means Shrive, a penance, for the Suns disappearance during the winter months, causing hardship as crops et al perish in the cold. This festival coincides with Lent which means Lengthening, the days get longer in length as we enter spring and the Sun comes into its power extending the daylight hours! (Hour = Horus, the Egyptian Sun-God). And when we drink the popular brand of orange juice namely Capri-Sun it really derives from the Egyptian word Khepri which is the morning sun. Even the celebration of father's day occurs on the summer solstice (21st June in the UK) and is nothing more or less than sun worship.

The word 'sun' and 'son' are one in the same, deriving from the German word 'Sonne', therefore when we say the Son of God we are also saying the Sun of God! The solar sun has a frequency of 126 hertz which is the frequency of unity consciousness and this is also referred to as Brahman consciousness. It is a state of consciousness where the ever-present witness is not just recognized as the core self of one's existence, it is now perceived as the primary reality of every experience. You, as the observer, are that pure consciousness.

Jesus watches over us from the skies supported by his disciples as they form heavenly government and continue their sermons in the form of the celestial narrative from the skies above. So from the Earthly Christ, which is an allegory of all of us and our internal genetic universe, we get the resurrected and heavenly Jesus, the solar Sun and the light of the world. It is a form of literary genius to have been able to fool so many people all over the world for many thousands of years in such a way that it controls their very essence and existence here on Earth still over 2000 years later on. And it is not a popular move to point it out and inform billions of people that they have been deceived!

Even the New Age hasn't been missed by the great deception. In these circles the heavenly Christ is called Sananda which in Sanskrit means 'Aspect of Lakshmi' which in Hindu is the feminine aspect of the Sun and the goddess of wealth, wealth from the sun meaning knowledge. Even within the New Age there are also many sayings blindly spoken such as the equivalent 'Peace be with you' among Church goers, in the New Age it is 'Love & Light'. But as I have pointed out numerous times with the various denominations of religions, all are different branches of the same tree, the bark of which will always have the same origin, the branches of which will be a seemingly different belief system, but it isn't... And that also goes for the 'New Age'. The phrase Love and Light has its origins in Freemasonry, in fact the 18th degree of the Scottish Rite of Freemasonry and the 'Order of the Golden Dawn' who have the saying, 'Love, Light, Life' from where the New Age has borrowed it. This was confirmed by an initiate of the Golden Dawn who contacted me recently after I had written about this subject on social media. It is Free-masonic magic and Sun worship! It emanates from the exact same old tree bark! But they have also been deceived in gigantic proportions and so have everyone and the facts speak for themselves.

And now for the greatest mystery the world has ever seen, Egypt and the Pyramids! I am now taking you back in time as the mystery is finally solved for you in the next chapter.

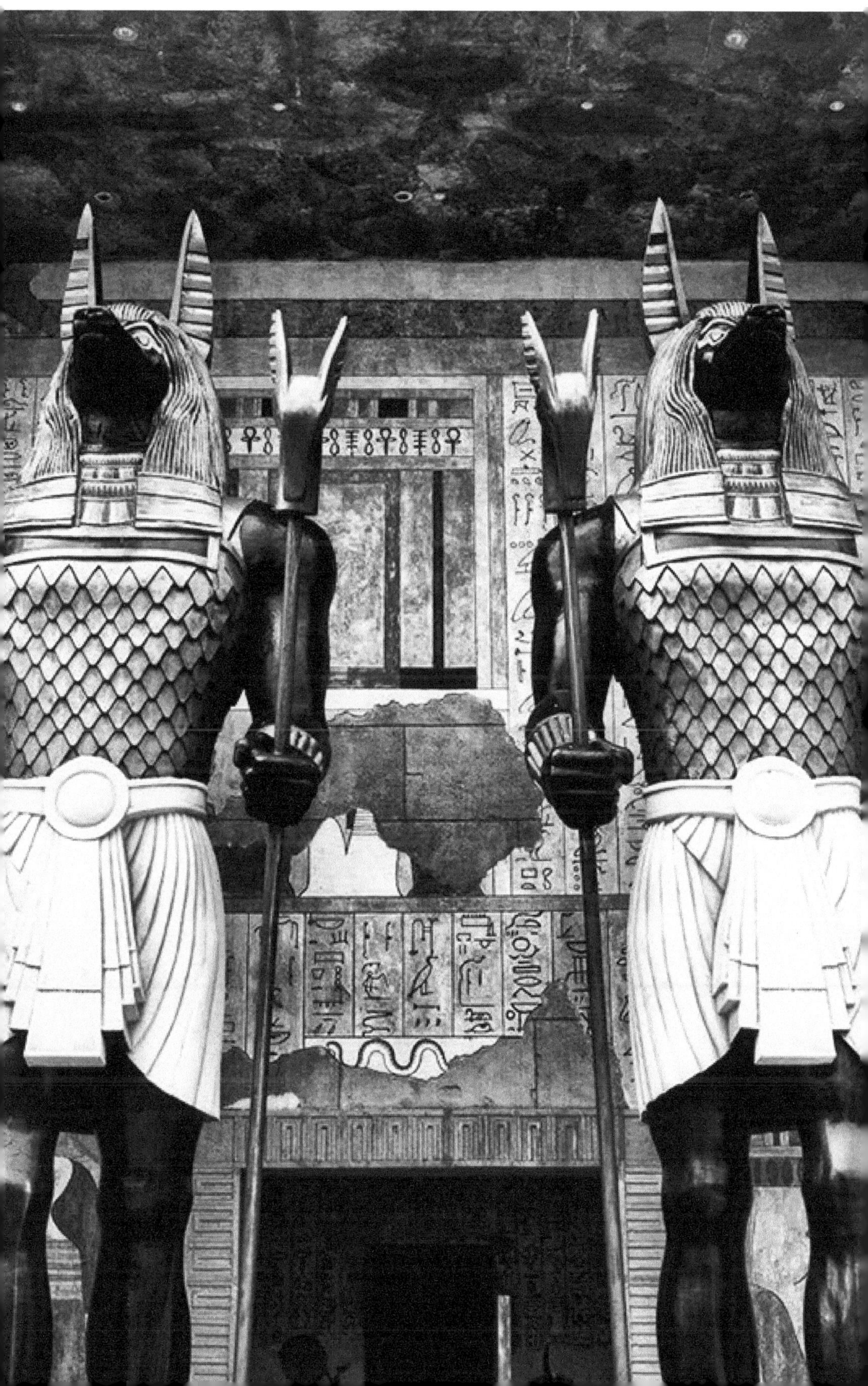

13

Hwt-Ka-Ptah: The Pyramid Code – The Mystery Solved

It was 2010 and Sarah and I were considering where to go on holiday that year and both of us were getting a strong urge to go to Egypt. We had a strong feeling that although this was under the guise of a vacation there were bigger things at work and it felt like a working holiday for us. So we gave into those urges and booked the holiday and also several internal trips whilst we were there including an internal flight to see the Museum of Cairo, the Nile and of course the main event the Pyramids. But in the weeks leading up to the holiday there was to be a deep spiritual twist that came entirely out of the blue for us.

We received an email from a psychic medium in Scotland, UK, who said that she had a message for us from her spiritual council. That message was *"with regards to your trip to Egypt, you must look passed the tourism, understand her, learn about her and then teach about her, a messenger will find you".* This added credence to our gut feeling that this was more than just the usual interesting holiday and that there was something more going on and hidden forces were at work, something was being planned ahead, something for us to do or to learn about. I now teach about the secrets of Egypt by virtue of books like this and talking events around the UK and even radio shows but at the time in 2010 it didn't really mean that much to me, only 7 years on does it make sense and only 7 years on has it become relevant in my life. It had been in waiting for all that time, fermenting inside me.

So the time had arrived and we landed on Egyptian soil in the blistering winter heat, trips booked and at the ready. The day had arrived for us to take a 4am flight to Cairo and that day was to be a memory forged forever as we visited the museum in Cairo seeing Mummy's over 3000 years old that looked better than me since I'd had an early start that day! Ancient artefacts like King Tutankhamun's death mask shone out at us in their golden splendour, lunch on the Nile and camel rides for some before the main spectacle, the Pyramids. As we drove around Cairo in our coach, packed with tourists, I lost count of the near misses with the bumper to bumper traffic, horses and other wandering animals. But then I saw what I had come to see, through the gaps in the building line the most familiar shape associated with this land, the tetrahedron Pyramid in all its glory adjacent to McDonalds as modern day capitalism stood shoulder to shoulder with ancient giants. I jumped off the coach having heard mainstream renditions of the reasons for the Pyramids, burial tombs the most recited but I knew this was completely incorrect. I eventually passed beggars and corrupt officials as I made my way to the Great pyramid and ventured inside for a brush with claustrophobia as I twisted and turned inside the narrow spaces. Then after soaking in many thousands of years of history in minutes of modern time, I made my way towards the guardian, the Sphinx, the route taken by many ancient initiates of the mystery schools of advanced knowledge and wisdom, a route walked with a sense of inner familiarity across the desert sands, desert deriving from the Egyptian word Deshret (DSHRT) meaning red lands.

What can be said about Egypt, it holds the key to greatness encrypted within the design of its monuments that many scholars and Egyptologists have tried to decode some getting much closer than others. I often sit there and smile as I witness theory after theory, guess after guess and question after question that I know the answer to, I was chosen to know and chosen to teach about Egypt! Within recent months I have been visited by Egyptian scarab beetles that manifested in front of me out of thin air, a serpent of light that scurried away from my feet and across the floor and even a Pharaoh of Egypt in full face covering headdress that just appeared and was walking along side me. I was able to see him from a left hand side view, from a morphed view as if I was looking out of the Pharaoh's eyes through my own face and even a head on view all at the same time simultaneously in a multidimensional experience. I am deeply connected to the land of Egypt and it sent a Pharaonic messenger who travelled through time to connect with me emanating out of a time and space portal that I heard manifesting.

In this chapter I am going to reveal to you the information that I have been entrusted to reveal to you because now is the time that Egypt wants to be revealed and resurrected again and I can feel her power bursting through the surface tension. The secrets left for us to find within the Pyramids especially, but also in other Egyptian artefacts, are a game changer for those who wish to learn and apply the sacred knowledge.

I have offered this information to the likes of the museum of Cairo and other Egyptian teaching establishments in the UK and elsewhere but unsurprisingly they were not interested. I guess when your livelihood depends upon mistruth you don't want to rock your own boat. But the waves of truth will eventually push that boat to the rocks of destruction. So it is now time to solve the mysteries that have captured the minds of men for thousands of years as I present to you the principle of soul science in pyramidal architectural form that is representing the anatomy of the human consciousness system of the brain. It is telling us of a neuropsychological awakening.

(Third eye chakra)

For those with the knowledge of mind and matter such as the Pharaohs and the Priesthoods life would have been a different experience. They believed themselves to be physical incarnations of the Sun-Gods, they were the walking knowledge also believing that such sacred knowledge was an honour and a privilege and not a general right. It had to be earned which has been the underlying principle of the higher society levels of the ancients throughout history. And this is still true of today amongst the priesthoods and the brotherhoods and the higher ranks of the societies with secrets (secret societies). They knew about and had a deep understanding of body and mind, the universe, genetics, harmonics and consciousness and how to attain the God-state of being, travelling out of body to what they deemed the 'other world'.

In order to know these things the Egyptians must have had access to the sophisticated scientific equipment used today in the 21st century or even had access to a greater knowledge base that they could tap into to retrieve such insight. They knew that in order to reach divinity the balance of opposites, namely duality, had to take place. They needed to bring equilibrium to the material and physical realm with harmony in order to be able to transcend out of it. They saw the physical and metaphysical as the two lands balanced by the sema-tawy from where we get the word cemetery, as the two worlds meet through ourselves from our transition from physical life to physical death. They knew about chemistry and alchemy which both derive from Al-khem meaning the way of Egypt. The two opposites of duality were to be balanced by the chemical marriage of King and Queen referred to as 'Tying the Knot' a phrase used today in modern day wedding ceremonies but without any idea of its origin.

(Tying The Knot)

Egyptian culture, like many other cultures past and present, had an array of Gods but what many people see as a religious theme is actually, unbeknown to them, a cryptic and sacred allegory and the Egyptian Gods were representations of what I am about to discuss in this chapter. The Gods and Goddess that appear mostly in this chapter are as follows:

Horus – Is the sun at dawn from where we get the word horizon (Horus-Risen) and also the word hour or hours (anagram of Horus). He is also the Thalamus and part of the human third eye endocrine system which I will detail later on.

RA – Means Sun in Egyptian, I discuss both RA and Amun RA in this chapter which is both the visible sun and the hidden sun within us

Set – Is the sunset which is the story of St George and the dragon (Apophis) and their battle as night approaches and the sun disappears into the duat (underworld escorted by the Akeru the Lion guardians) to return victorious at sunrise after their night time battle.

Osiris – He is known as the God of the staircase referring to the chakra system, he is also associated with the constellation Orion and God of the underworld which I detail later. He is also the Pineal gland of the human third eye system which is significant when we get to the great pyramid a little later on.

Isis – The goddess of motherhood associated with both Sirius 'A' and the Moon. She is the Pituitary gland of the human third eye system which again becomes more relevant when we reach the great pyramid later in this chapter.

Thoth – The god of wisdom, his name is really a metaphor for 'thought' and again when we reach the pyramids this will become clearer.

Wadjet – Seen on the headdress of King Tutankhamun and other Pharaohs and ruler of Lower Egypt, meaning north of the Nile delta. Cats were revered in Egypt as they can see into the two worlds and they had several cat goddess such as Wadjet. Cats also purr at a frequency range of 20-140 hertz which is a frequency range of healing.

Nehkbet – Again seen on King Tutankhamun's headdress and ruler of Upper Egypt, south of the Nile delta. The Pharaoh was seen as the balancer of the two lands and ruler of both combined and the balance of opposites is pinnacle as you will see later.

Anubis – Meaning Royal child, Egyptian myth tells us that he was the offspring of Osiris and Nephthys, who presented herself as Isis herself (Nephthys means invisible sister) who in astronomy is Sirius B. The word sister derives from the phrase 'Isis-Star'. Anubis escorted souls to the underworld to be judged by Osiris.

There are of course many other Gods and Goddesses but I have concentrated on those of relevance to the secret code revealed within this book.

The whole concept of Royal which means God-Kings and Royalty stems from the Pharaohs of Egypt who believed themselves to be the walking sun gods. Even the physical crown worn by monarchs is symbolic of the crown chakra within our head and the crown chakra is a cosmic connector. We have a Monarchy which derives from Moon-Arch, the Moon being Isis. The Isis means 'she of the throne' and as the Pituitary gland she is throne/seat of the mind. Osiris means Throne/seat of the soul and as the Pineal gland he is throne/seat of the soul, I will go a little more into detail about this later on in this chapter.

The Queen of England sits on a throne that is full of Egyptian symbolism and the whole theme of interbreeding marriages also comes from ancient Egypt where husband and wife were usually brother and sister and even the linage of their bloodline can be traced back to Egypt too and so can all but one American President. So when we hear of Royal marriages between Prince's and commoners this is not true and cannot be, it is against internal etiquette. And the forthcoming wedding of Prince Harry and Megan Markel is a prime example. The streets will be lined with the flag of St George (which is really Egyptian and not English) waving ignorantly at another Royal wedding as camera's pan over the homeless for this ceremony of pomp and grandeur at our expense!

(Rachel) Megan Markel, the new bride of Prince Harry thinks that Ancient and Royal Bloodlines are "Mumbo Jumbo" (her words). But just who is this new Royal Princess? She is descended from the House of Du Pont, an elite European Illuminati bloodline, on her father's side. She is also related to King's Richard the Lionheart (She was born with the Sun in Leo which is the Lion King) and King John, both of Nottingham's Robin Hood fame. And where was her first Royal public appearance?... Yes it was Nottingham! She was given a blood test to confirm her eligibility to join this Royal House of David (Judaism) and passed, otherwise the marriage would simply not be happening. The Royal family will only mix with its own bloodline and this cannot change and as stated this goes back to ancient Egypt and the Pharaohs. So when we hear the media claiming the likes of the other Princess, Kate Middleton being a commoner, it is a complete fabrication! They are all related and always will be, it is a way of ensuring that only Royal blood mixes together and doesn't get contaminated by common blood.The whole thing as per usual is a complete arranged set-up so enjoy the wedding and let's all send our congratulations.

Egypt is also engrained into modern society especially the likes of America, Paris and London. Some of examples of this are the Obelisk and Glass Pyramid in central Paris, Big Ben which is the Benebenet, the pyramid capstone, situated at the Houses of Parliament and the river Thames deriving from Tamas meaning dark river, now representing apophis, the opposer of light, which was formerly known as Isis, the river Goddess all of which are situated in central London.

The seat motifs within the House of Commons are the Hoshen which was the breast plate of the serpent priests of Osiris (Djedhi). The Djedhi, the Serpent Priests (Serpent representing Wisdom) and initiates of the ancient mystery schools of Egypt were the protectors of the Temple of Osiris, indicated by the Djed (spine of Osiris symbolising strength). They later became the Druids of the British Isles, Druid meaning 'Oak Knowledge' (Tree knowledge). The Djed is the spine (Jacobs Ladder) and at the top of the spine is the head, the Temple, which means 'House of God' and house means Mind! So in other words the Djedhi (Jedi for you StarWars fans) were the protectors of the sacred knowledge of consciousness which they brought to Britain from Egypt. And of course the river Thames itself is Apophis the dark serpent who caused famine in Egypt by swallowing the water of the Nile. His head is where the O2 arena is now situated (O2 = Oxygen). Apophis is the opposer of light and the enemy of Isis. Even the three city of London police stations are set out to the shape of the constellation of Orion's belt (Orion is associated with Osiris).

Then we get to America (Am-Erica = the rule of the eternal Eagle) which is rife with Egyptian symbology and meaning. The declaration of independence signed on the 4th July was significant by virtue of the fact that on 4th July Sirius 'A' is furthest away from the solar sun and the founding fathers wishes to commemorate this invisibility into their history. It was signed in Philadelphia, Philae is where the temple of Isis is situated in Egypt and Delphi means Delphos which is the womb, Isis is the Goddess of motherhood and this is also signified by the Dome shaped buildings in the likes of Washington DC (District of Columbia, Columbia is a form of Isis) and of course the obelisk, the corner stone of which was erected at the exact time Sirius 'A' passed overhead at precisely 10:59am on August 7th 1880. The statue of liberty which was originally destined for Egypt, from where the enligthenment of the world will emanate, is Isis and her flame is Horus, these characters are Semiramis and Nimrod in Babylon. But nevertheless it represents the masonic enlightenment of the world, hence the 7 rays from liberties head which are symbolic of the enlightened mind. It is Sirius 'A' and the solar sun. The ancient capital of Egypt was Memphis which means 'White Walls' and this is why America has a White House! Within the White House there is the 'Oval Office' again referring to the womb and fertility of Isis. Even the good old Hotdog is Egyptian. In July and August the sun was so hot that the Egyptians would try and appease the heat, they believed that Sirius 'A' gave the sun its power and therefore they would sacrifice a dog to Sirius (the dog star) called 'dog days'. The hotdog is symbolic of this canine ritual sacrifice.

When the Queen attends the London cenotaph (obelisk/symbol of Osiris) on Remembrance Day (remembrance also meaning token/souvenir) dressed in black this signifies the God of the underworld Osiris who is judge of the soul. He is also associated with the colour black. There is also the planet Saturn connotations too of course.

The Egyptians knew and understood the workings of our most inner-self and they practiced wholeness and divinity reaching the dizzy heights of enlightenment. They knew how to find and extract knowledge and wisdom from their own DNA/RNA that we can only do now by way of sophisticated and advanced technical scientific equipment, that we are told is a product of the 21st century.

There were 3 main pyramids at Giza, The great pyramid which is Khufu's pyramid (Khufu means 'Name of a Pharaoh' and in numerology this name has an expression/core number of 22, which is the number I continue to frequently see), Khafre's pyramid (Khafre is a variant of Khufu) and Menkaure's pyramid (Menkaure means 'Divine'). The Egyptians had a quadrant system of consciousness which were as follows: They were Osiris, Isis and Horus as the Pineal gland, pituitary gland and the Thalamus and the Cerebellum: situated as part of the endocrine system of the human brain.

(Endocrine Third Eye System)

PINEAL GLAND: Osiris

The pineal gland, also known as the pineal body, conarium or epiphysis cerebri, (also relevant to the religious celebration called Epiphany

(Epiphysis - meaning Pineal Gland, which is an ancient Christian feast day and is significant in a number of ways, celebrating the baptism of Jesus by John the Baptist, which was in the River Jordan/Spinal Fluid). The life of John the Baptist prepared the way for the Christ seed and his death was symbolic of death of the old and former you to become the new Christ consciousness you. The Pineal is a small endocrine gland in the vertebrate brain. The shape of the gland resembles a pine cone, hence its name. The pineal gland is located in the epithalamus, near the centre of the brain, between the two hemispheres, tucked in a groove where the two halves of the thalamus join. The pineal gland produces melatonin, a serotonin derived hormone which modulates sleep patterns in both circadian and seasonal cycles. The Pineal Gland (face of God, from Hebrew story of Jacob fighting the Angel of Mount Penial) is also known as the 'Inner Light' which is indicated in Hindu by the Bindi placed as a 'Red Dot' between the physical eyes and in Egypt by the 'Black Dot' the Aten. And also the Hathor headdress, Hathor meaning House of Horus, the inner light, symbolised by the Egyptian sun between cow horns. The pineal gland also connects us to Earth's night and day cycles (Chronobiology cycles) secreting melatonin at night time which helps rejuvenate and rebirths us. If for example you work nights then you are in a permanent state of a death cycle as the body dies in the day and is reborn at night (cell production etc). If you are awake during normal sleep times then you cannot rejuvenate. It is stated by modern medical history that the existence of the Pineal gland has been known for circa 2000 years. The Egyptians knew about its existence many thousands of years prior to that! This gland secretes (from where we get the word secret) White & Brown fluids which was hidden within Judaism with the term for Israel, the 'Land of Milk and Honey'.

PITUITARY GLAND: Isis

The pituitary gland, or hypophysis, is an endocrine gland about the size of a pea (where we get the expression Pea Brain) and weighing 0.5 grams (0.018 oz) in humans. It is a protrusion off the bottom of the hypothalamus at the base of the brain. The hypophysis rests upon the hypophysial fossa of the sphenoid bone in the center of the middle cranial fossa and is surrounded by a small bony cavity (sella turcica) covered by a dural fold (diaphragm) sellae). The anterior pituitary (or adenohypophysis) is a lobe of the gland that regulates several physiological processes (including stress, growth, reproduction, and lactation). The intermediate lobe synthesizes and secretes melanocyte-stimulating hormone. The posterior pituitary (or neurohypophysis) is a lobe of the gland that is functionally connected to the hypothalamus by the median eminence via a small tube called the pituitary stalk (also called the infundibular stalk or the infundibulum). Hormones secreted from the pituitary gland help control: growth, blood pressure, certain functions of the sex organs, thyroid glands and metabolism as well as some aspects of pregnancy, childbirth (Represented by Isis, Goddess of Motherhood), nursing, water/salt concentration at the kidneys, temperature regulation and pain relief. The Pituitary Gland also deals with fertility and lactation, hence another reason it is associated with Isis the Mother Goddess. The section between the Pineal and Pituitary Gland is called the 'Crystal Palace' for all you London football fans out there!

THALAMUS: Horus

The Thalamus (from Greek θάλαμος, "chamber") is the large mass of grey matter in the dorsal part of the diencephalon of the brain with several functions such as relaying of sensory and motor signals to the cerebral cortex, and the regulation of consciousness, sleep, and alertness. It is a midline symmetrical structure of two halves, within the vertebrate brain, situated between the cerebral cortex and the midbrain. The medial surface of the two halves constitute the upper lateral wall of the third ventricle. It is the main product of the embryonic diencephalon and it works with our Amygdala (Mary Magdalene).

CEREBELLUM: (which also deals with equilibrium)

The cerebellum (Latin for "little brain") is a major feature of the hindbrain of all vertebrates. Although usually smaller than the cerebrum. In humans, the cerebellum plays an important role in motor control, and it may also be involved in some cognitive functions such as attention and language as well as in regulating fear and pleasure responses but its movement-related functions are the most solidly established. The human cerebellum does not initiate movement, but contributes to coordination, precision, and accurate timing: it receives input from sensory systems of the spinal cord and from other parts of the brain, and integrates these inputs to fine-tune motor activity. Cerebellar damage produces disorders in fine movement, equilibrium, posture, and motor learning in humans.

(The Death Mask of King Tutankhamun)

King Tutankhamun's (Tut-Ankh-Amun meaning strong and secret Genes, when we separate the words individually) Death Mask (which I saw at the Cairo Museum) illustrates several things given to us in plain sight. The rear of the headdress is the Cerebellum and our brain stem.

The front of the mask also shows the Cerebellum and its Lateral wings, separated by the Vermis, the serpent. It also shows the Vulture Goddess of Upper Egypt, Nekhbet and the Goddess of Lower Egypt, Wadjet, symbolic of the merging of the two lands, Upper and Lower Egypt by King Tutankhamun who was Pharaoh of both lands. The chin décor is the Uraeus or Greek Oura, meaning tail, in this case the tail of the serpent. The head of the serpent is masculine and the Tail is feminine, again we see the merging of opposites, masculine and feminine energy. We also have the serpent wisdom emanating from the third eye, the Pineal Gland, between the right and left eye, again opposites, male and female aspects of bodily control. The mysterious earrings worn by a male Pharoah simply means the balance of masculine and feminine.

(The Scarab Beetle depicting wings of the Cerebellum)

The Scarab beetle also represents the Lateral wings of the Cerebellum and the hemispheres and the Aten, the Inner Sun/Light.

The 3 Wise-men are all overseen by the Cerebellum, the Bishop (meaning watcher/overseer) sitting on the Seat (Cathedral means seat/Energy seat/ chakras) and many Cathedrals once the human head is overlayed on their diagrams, show in a clandestine way the locations of these 3 endocrine glands, as does the greatest monuments of them all, the Great Pyramid.

Giza meaning 'border', representing Upper and Lower Egypt, North and South of the Nile Delta were merged by the Mind – Memphis, the symbolic Mind, with Heliopolis being the Heart and Thebes being the Tongue, HTM, Heart, Tongue and Mind. Memphis was the original capital city. And in line with frequencies, the Great Pyramids of Giza harness the very sound waves from the inner core of the earth which coincides with alpha The rhythms produced by the human brain during meditation. The pyramids, Earth and the brain have the same range of frequencies. This is an advanced knowledge of sound/vibrational frequencies.

THE ANKH:

The Ankh, the key of Life which is really the process of 'DNA and Protein

Synthesis. Protein synthesis is the biological generation of cells that bind with DNA. When protein binds with DNA it loops and crosses around and over it and bonds in loop shapes before closing itself and tying itself off which is symbolised in the Ankh shape. The Ankh, key of life, is referring to DNA/Life DNA synthesis is the expansion and creation through the double helix DNA system of reproduction and revitalising of genetics, which again is essential within the term life. The two serpents represent the Ida and Pingala (kundalini energy) travelling up the spine (Jacobs ladder) towards the Cerebellum hemispheres (wings) and the Aten (Pineal Gland, the Inner light) RA is the visible Sun (Sun-God) but the Amun RA is our hidden light, (hidden Sun) our inward journey to divinity and wisdom accessed through the invisible doors of our own Pyramid, to be activated into cosmic consciousness.

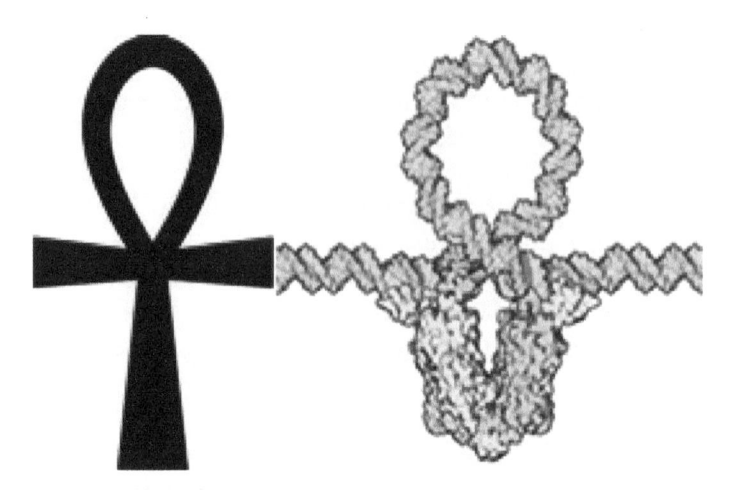

(Egyptian Ankh and DNA Synthesis)

And that leads nicely onto the Pyramids themselves in the desert of Giza. So what were these monuments all about? In acknowledgement that there are many other Pyramids around the world and indeed beyond, I will concentrate on Giza in Egypt.

So what have the scholars and Egyptologists of every decade and age missed?

When we watch TV documentaries about Egypt and the Pyramid and Sphinx of Giza (Giza meaning border) and are told that they were built for the burials of the Pharaoh's by Hebrew slaves who worked with primitive tools to carrying rocks and stones hundreds of tons in weight over rough terrain non-stop for 20 plus years, are we being deluded or deliberately deceived by the same groups and organisations that have tried to keep certain information a secret? They know that the flux of enlightenment and the increase in the wisdom of humanity will come with the re-emergence of Egyptian knowledge and they are trying to stop it from occurring.

This knowledge has stood the test of time and has been left written in the constructs of the Pyramids and Sphinx for us to decipher, it is a coded message of the grandest scale missed by the thousands of tourists who visit them each year only seeing, as I was told not to, the tourism of this great land and not her cosmic reconnecting message. The Pyramids of Giza were not for burials at all, that occurred in Luxor (Luxor meaning Golden Light) in the Valley of the Kings. Many, including Napoleon himself, have experienced strangeness when they ventured into certain places such as the Sarcophagus, they experience an almost out of body, astral travel like imagery, enabled by the remnants of such ancient rehearsals and practices and gateways unsealed. They are experiencing the merging of two lands, the physical and metaphysical as aspects of themselves leave for a while, as to where, only those who travel there really know. The Pyramids are in essence a giant replica of the human brain and its endocrine system of enlightenment. This is the message that has been left for us to find: it is a massive statement (state of mind) left for us on the landscape telling us how to make that transition from man to the God-like mind.

The Sphinx is the guardian of this sacred knowledge that initiates must first pass in order to venture any further into truth. The Sphinx faces due east which in cardinal points represents enlightenment and illumination, exactly what it protects, Egyptian Mummies also face east. The Sphinx stands at 240 feet long and 66 feet tall. In Greek Sphinx means Sphingo to restrict as in their version of the Riddle of the Sphinx with those who fail being strangled. If we use the mathematical formula of 240 divided by 66 we get 3.6363636364 which I would guess are the coordinates to somewhere, but as yet I don't know where. In Arabic it translates as 'father of dread' but dread has several meanings, the meanings most apt in this case are to 'regard with great awe or reverence' a synonym of which is to stand in awe of or regard with awe. However in Egyptian Sphinx means 'to combine' and this is relevant in several ways as such. As part of enlightenment the Egyptians were combining opposites into one. The Sphinx is a mythical creature with a lion's body and a human head. This is relevant because the Sun, which is symbolised by a lion, activates the endocrine system within the human head and as we can see the Sphinx has the serpent headdress that is associated with the cerebellum, the fourth aspect of the Egyptian quadrant system of consciousness.

(The Sphinx - Giza in Egypt – Guardian of Sacred Knowledge)

The human brain has four regions/chambers namely the 'Ventricles' the four fluid filled chambers filled with Cerebral Spinal Fluid. The brain also

has Four Regions: They are:
Cerebrum,

Diencephalon,

Cerebellum,

Brain stem

The brain also has 4 lobes one of which is the Occipital lobe which are lobes that are pyramid-shaped structures located at the back of the brain that receive and analyse visual information!

The great pyramid of Giza has four chambers, chamber meaning an enclosed space or room, namely:

The Kings chamber,

The Queens chamber,

The Grand gallery

The Lower gallery

The King's chamber and Queen's chamber are connected by the grand gallery, a bridge, or in the anatomy of the brain a 'Pons' meaning bridge, they are neural pathways or tracts that conduct signals from the brain down to the cerebellum and medulla, and tracts that carry the sensory signals up into the Thalamus and they connect the cerebellum to the pons and midbrain. Again this is the inner most workings of our mind. There is a tower within the Kings chamber which is symbolic of the Djed, the spine of Osiris. The top of the spine gives us the head and the consciousness arena.

In standard spiritual circles there are 7 chakras of the human body However the Egyptian based theirs on 9, with the addition of the Nasal chakra and the Carnal chakra and it is therefore no surprise that we have

9 Pyramids situated in the Giza Plateau. The carnal chakra is the skin and is symbolic of the outer projection of our inner truths. The nasal chakra is our olfactory consciousness through smell. Nikola Tesla once said *"If you only knew the magnificence of the 3, 6 and 9, then you would have a key to the universe"* and this is relevant because there are 9 pyramids in sets of 3 which give us 3, 6 and 9, within this the Egyptians were giving us the harmonic keys to the universe. It is factor 9 universal harmonics as frequencies are divisible by 9. The 9 levels of consciousness is a model of how the physical and none physical universe work together, which is including of the material realm and the 9ether forces of creation, a magical marriage. Even the Mayan pyramid of 9 steps is secretly telling us of the 9 stages of consciousness, one stage for each step.:

1) Oversoul
2) Individual soul
3) Higher mind
4) Template level of reality
5) The collective unconscious
6) The individual unconscious
7) Beliefs
8) Emotions
9) Thoughts

The cross, amongst other meanings both genetic and astronomical, indicates the number 9 as such, which is the 9 chakra system:

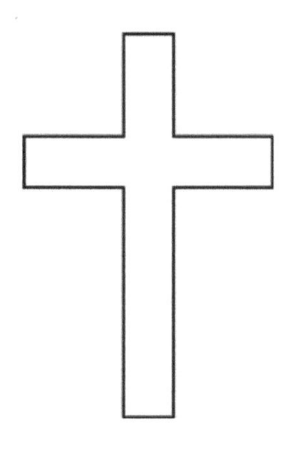

```
        9
    8   6   7
        5
        4
        3
        2
        1
```

(6-7-8 are the three component parts of the third eye, the Essenbach code)

Everything in creation is a smaller version of the larger, the microcosm, macrocosm Russian doll effect and whereas the human body has an energy meridian system, so do countries and so do planets, they all have meridian Leylines (Ley means law, and the line is the sacred shape of the partition). When we look at the African Prime-Meridian chakra system we can see that Giza is its third eye:

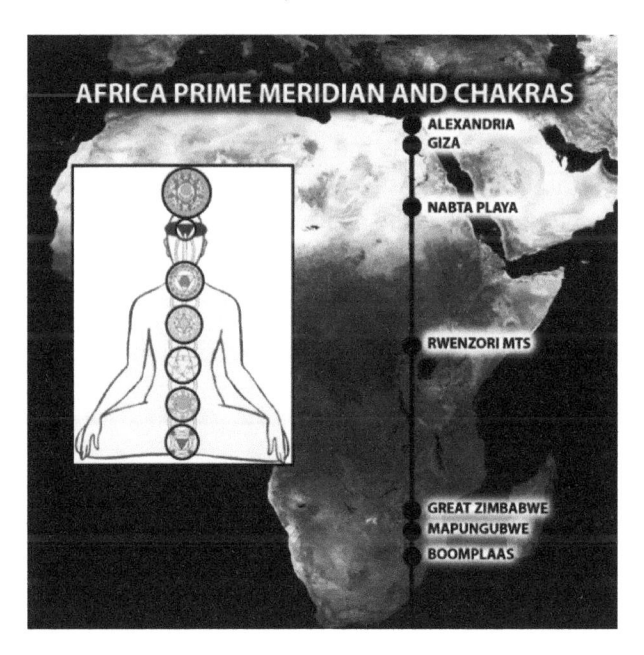

(Africa Prime-Meridian Chakra System)

Alexandria which took over from Memphis as the eventual capital of Egypt is the Crown Chakra in this African meridian (Golden Pyramid Cap) It has been proven that the Sphinx and Pyramids were once surrounded by water (Nile River – Nile means Yeor which is to shine and from where we get the word year). The Pituitary Gland shines with the same luminescence and that is no coincidence. Water erosion has been found beneath these monuments however water has not been in this region for 10,000 years, therefore the Sphinx at least and most likely the Pyramids must be at least this old, bearing in mind that 10,000 year old star maps have been discovered within the Great pyramid of Egypt.

Within the brain we have the water that surrounds and protects the brain called the Cerebrospinal fluid that comes into direct contact with our brains third ventricle and therefore the pineal Gland. It transports thoughts and information via Neuro-hormones and bio-chemical signalling to all parts of the body down this fluid system, which is what this picture of Thoth (Thought) is representing: Christ consciousness is a higher level of thought and the word Thoth derives from the word thought. Thought neurons sometimes called ground neurons pass on environmental information which is also knowledge, which is stored within parts of the brain. Ground consciousness is the eighth of eight consciousness and is the basis or ground for the rising of all other consciousness. It is also a cognitive consciousness. It is the final awakening. The eight consciousness are collections of consciousness, namely:

1. Visual.

2. Auditory.

3. Olfactory.

4. Gustatory.

5. Tactile.

6. Mental.

7. Defiled mental consciousness or emotional consciousness.

8. All ground consciousness, Final awakening.

They then transform into the five wisdoms:

1. Alaya (basis) into wisdom.

2. Alaya consciousness into mirror like wisdom reflecting everything.

3. Emotional consciousness into wisdom of equality which reflects good or bad.

4. Mental consciousness into wisdom of discernment.

5. Five sense consciousness into all accomplishing wisdom.

Neurons are a brain to body conveyance of information. Thoughts and actions are encoded in the activity of neurons. It is an electrical signature of thoughts and actions. Fired by an electrical signal. Thoth was the God of wisdom and you can now see why.

(Thought/Thoth travelling along the Cerebrospinal fluid on his solar boat which is biophotons)

The Monkey is symbolic of the Olfactory Tract in the brain that bears similarity to a Monkey. The Olfactory Tract a nerve like, white band composed primarily of nerve fibres originating from the mitral cells and tufted cells of the olfactory bulb but also containing the scattered cells of the anterior olfactory nucleus. The tract, closely applied to the inferior surface of the frontal lobe, attaches itself to the base of the cerebral hemisphere at the olfactory trigone, beyond which it extends in the form of the olfactory striae that distribute their fibres to the olfactory tubercle and, in largest number, to the olfactory cortex on and around the uncus of the parahippocampal gyrus. It also deals with the sense of smell and this activates olfactory consciousness. The Olfactory Tract is a nervous system messenger.

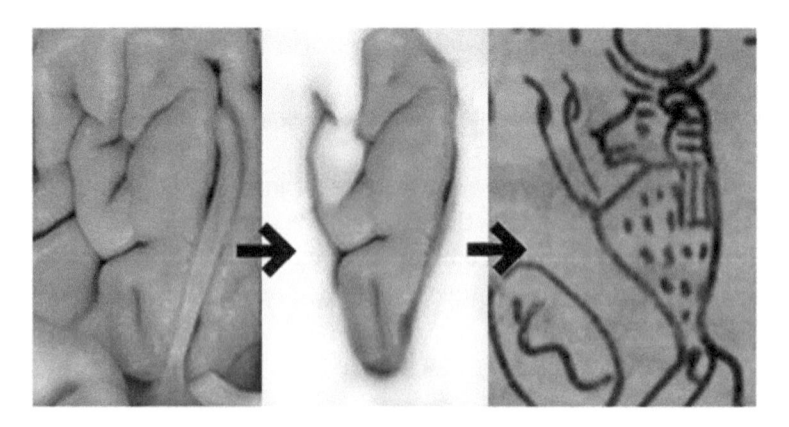

(Olfactory Tract of the Brain & Egyptian Picture)

The Pyramids were so placed as to replicate the waters of the Cerebrospinal fluids that also surround our endocrine third eye system. This was all in line with the mastering of opposites which leads to enlightenment and divinity the Pyramids and their structure is also very relevant to this fact.

Water is an information carrier that changes blood (turning water to wine) reflecting the character of consciousness. Water and thoughts are comprised of the same things and the energy of mind will structure water. When water is freezing or at the point of freezing excess energy is extracted from the water and at this point the molecules start to spin and link together in a pattern of the tetrahedron and water then develops a consciousness. The tetrahedron shape is the model of consciousness. Even the element of fire has a tetrahedron as its symbol.

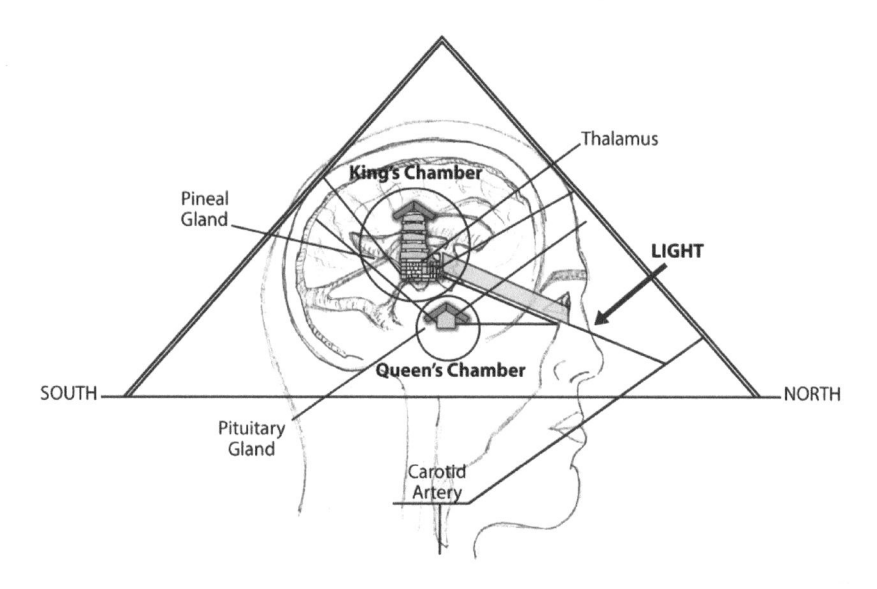

(Overlay of the Great Pyramid with the Human brain)

When we overlay the human head (facing North-North gate (pineal gland) we can see that it marks the different parts of the third eye endocrine system of consciousness. The Pineal gland is where the King's chamber is situated. The Pituitary gland is where the Queen's chamber is situated and also within these we have the position of the Thalamus. These are the 3 master glands of consciousness. Enlightened consciousness processes. The Great pyramid is the anatomy of the brain and its master gland consciousness functions. The merging of our opposites is the alchemical marriage of King and Queen which merge together as one in the Thalamus. Therefore, the Pineal Gland (Osiris), the Pituitary Gland (Isis) and the Thalamus (Horus) become one. It is no coincidence then that within the Great Pyramid we have the King's chamber, Queen's chamber and the Thalamus within this monument. The Great Pyramid is situated in the exact centre of Earth's land mass and the Thalamus is the centre of the brain. The solar sun is of course at the centre of our solar system.

The Pyramids as so shaped as to also represent what we have inside the brain called 'Pyramidal Neurons' which are by virtue of their name are pyramid shaped. Pyramid means fire in the middle and pyramidal neurons fire electrical signals from their centre (middle). We also have 'Mirror Neurons' which reflect each other and make each other aware of their own existence and therefore create consciousness which is aware of being aware. Pyramidal neurons deal with advanced cognitive functions which incorporates knowledge. This again is no coincidence and purely by advanced design.

The King's chamber (Pineal gland) vibrates at 8 hertz as do the alpha waves of the human brain which become more activate and excitable when the Pineal gland is awakened, it also causes an altered state of consciousness. I will mention 432 hertz again in a little while. 432 hertz resonates with 8 hertz expanding consciousness and enabling you to tune into universal knowledge. The two hemispheres of the brain are synchronised with each other at 8 hertz and this harmony causes maximum flow of information and is the key to activating full potential of the brain. 8 hertz also induces DNA replication and that takes us back to the ankh which is in itself symbolising DNA duplication and replication, the key of life and the key to life. The neo-cortex of the brain, the 90% unassigned, becomes awakened in this synchronization and one then operates in all brain cell dendrites with the maximum information flow possible on that scale. It reawakens us to the orchestra of our thoughts.

When we tune into universal knowledge and information everything that has previously been stored and imputed there can be used and accessed by others of that race. It is a morphogenetic grid of sorts. I think that the Egyptians and others used this method in the construction of their monuments and the secret and sacred knowledge that they encoded within them hiding in a secret place the knowledge of what they truly represent.

Not only, as previously mentioned, is 33 hertz the frequency of Christ consciousness, but it is aso a key activation frequency that sacred sites resonate at. It is also the most natural frequency of consciousness for humans. In geometry a pyramid is a polyhedron with five faces and is formed by connecting a polygonal base and a point called the apex. Each base edge and apex form a triangle called a lateral face which is a conic (cone) solid with a polygonal base. This is significant because it represents the number 5 which is the number of the 'realised man' and to become one. The number 5 is used repeatedly in the kings chamber, such as the number of levels of granite beams and hence chambers above the King chamber and the number of courses of masonry on the walls of the King's chamber. In geometry the number 5 is the pentagram which is also significant biblically with the 5 wounds of Christ which represent the same pentagram of the realised man. The inner angles of the pentagram = 108 degrees this turned into the frequency of 108 hertz is the frequency of 'total knowing' that speeds up spiritual development and the experience of an aletered state of consciousness. It is the hertz frequency that also connects you to the higher spiritual planes and a variant of this is 108,000 which is the associated value of the Kings chamber. I also think that the Egyptians and others were able to harness such sounds and frequencies to create lasers in which to cut the stones with minute precision and also use that sound to make the stones levitate.

This was most likely done by the chord F # which was also the vibration of the prayers sung by the priests inside the pyramids.

A team of researchers in Switzerland have developed a way of levitating and transporting objects using nothing but sound. Using ultrasonic waves that is, sound waves whose frequencies are too high for humans to hear, scientists at the Swiss Federal Institute of Technology in Zurich have made water droplets, instant coffee crystals, Styrofoam flakes, and a toothpick, among other objects, hang in mid-air, move along a plane, and interact with each other. It is the first time that scientists have been able to use sound to simultaneously levitate several objects next to each other and move them around. But it isn't the first time in my opinion, the Egyptians did it many thousands of years ago.

In 2010 researchers built sound lasers, coaxing a collection of phonons to travel together. But those first devices were hybrid models that used the light from a traditional laser to create a coherent sound emission. In traditional lasers, a bunch of electrons in a gas or crystal are excited all at the same time. When they relax back to their lower energy state, they release a specific wavelength of light, which is then directed with mirrors to produce a beam. Sound lasers work on a similar principle. A mechanical oscillator jiggles and excites a bunch of phonons, which relax and release their energy back into the device. The confined energy causes the phasor to vibrate at its fundamental frequency but with at a very narrow wavelength. The sound laser produces phonons at 170 kilohertz, far above human hearing range, which peters out around 20 kilohertz. The pyramids were resonance chambers.

It is also no coincidence that the Great pyramid had 144,000 outer casing stones and in gemetria, the numerical value of letters and words, 144 is light. 144 is the secret key and concept of light itself. The human third eye as a hertz frequency of, you guessed it, 144 hertz. The 144,000 outer cased Limestones caused the pyramid to gleam like a "light" in the bright sun and could be seen for many miles. Limestone (and its quartz frequencies) also line up with Christ Consciousness! Limestone also has the same approximate wavelength as Gold, which is the colour of enlightenment. Limestone and Gold are both around 590 NM (Nanometres).

Quartz is a mineral composed of silicon and oxygen atoms in a continuous framework of SiO_4 silicon–oxygen tetrahedral (pyramid shape), with each oxygen being shared between two tetrahedrons, giving an overall chemical formula of SiO_2. Quartz is the second most abundant mineral in Earth's continental crust, behind feldspar.

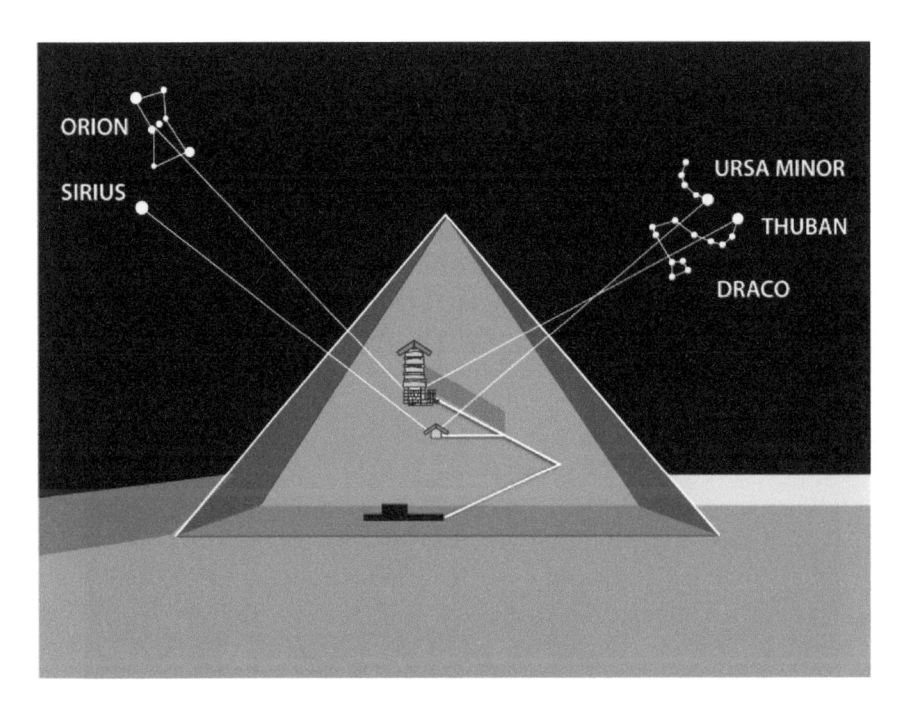

(The Great Pyramid shafts and their associated star constellations)

Even the much debated pyramid shafts were purposely directed at certain stars, and for good reason too. The Pineal Gland (King's chamber) within the Great Pyramid has a shaft that faces Orion (also Osiris, known as the shaft of Osiris) and the Pituitary Gland (Isis/known as the star chamber of Isis) faces Sirius A (also Isis) this is again the two opposites, male and female facing South. The shafts are star chambers. Both the King's and Queen's Chamber were built rectangular which symbolises stability. In the North (opposite of South facing shafts) we have two shafts facing Thuban in Ursa Minor and Draco, (The Pineal Gland is also known as the North Gate). This is why the Great pyramid is locked true north because the Pineal gland is the North gate.

Draco is now called the Dragon, however in ancient Egyptian times it was called the Cobra/serpent and it was one constellation. In higher dimensional terms the serpent/dragon is symbolic of going beyond or leaving the solid world, sheading its skin, like the soul does as it leaves the physical skin, the body which can be done either living or otherwise. The Egyptians did this in a physical living state most likely using knowledge given to them by a higher aspect of themselves which may have conversed with them in their out of body state. The head of the serpent represents the male and the tail represents the female aspect of self, two opposite sides. This is also known as the 'Draconian Traverse', traverse meaning to lie across. The Pyramid shape therefore is symbolic of two opposites mastered and merged as one as they reach the Pyramid capstone, where two become one and connect to divinity and enlightenment.

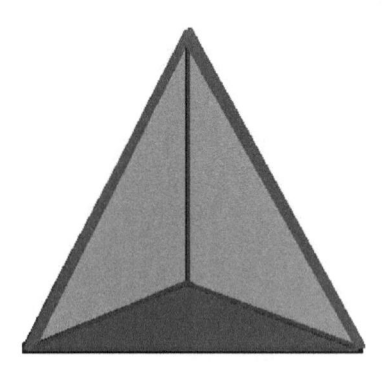

(The Tetrahedron)

The Pyramid, the alchemical symbol of fire, at its two bottom corners represent the two opposites merging into one at the Apex, the Gold Cap stone (Gold = symbolic of enlightenment), the Crown chakra. The pyramid base also represents the material/physical realm and the apex is a representation of the higher consciousness and the transit from one to the other.

The third eye will only open when 'conscious fusion' takes place between the opposites of our own consciousness. There would have been various initiations and rituals within the pyramids to induce this state, accessed most probably through the guardian of higher knowledge, the Sphinx. It was the transition from unconscious matter to conscious existence with the mastery of this world and its duality, which is the symbolic meaning behind the legendary Phoenix from the flames. They were reaching the mental state (Ment-Al = mind of God). The mind relates to the brain, the greater mind, the mental, relates to the higher consciousness state. So, in keeping with theme of the balance of opposites there are many Egyptian statues that are clearly holding onto two cylinder shaped metal rods, one in each hand. The foot position of these statues is also of relevance. When we see the left foot more prominently forward it's of matriarchal significance and when we see the right foot more prominently forward it's of patriarchal significance. But going back to the rods these are what are known as the 'Wands of Horus' and they were metal cylinders filled with various special materials and quartz crystals of differing sizes to enhance their psychic and mental ability as well as the balancing of their chakras, bringing harmony to their physical vessel and healing by regulating the energy balance of the body and they were a tool for attainment and unsurprisingly enlightenment.

The Wands of Horus take the form of two hollow cylinders made of copper and zinc for right and left hands respectively. This is important because the link between metal and hand is tightly bound up with the functions of the left and right hemispheres of the brain. Copper was held in the right hand and this symbolised the Sun (male energy) and the zinc was held in the left hand and this symbolised the Moon (female energy) and required the fundamental balance of the two.

(The Wands of Horus - Copper held in right hand, Zinc held in the left-the left foot forward means matriarchal system of balance)

All external and internal dimensions of the Wands of Horus conform strictly to the proportions of the Golden Section. This is of fundamental Importance for the existence of resonant interaction between the cylinders and the user. To work effectively the Wands of Horus need to attune themselves to the organism, while the user's organism for its part should also attune itself to the Wands of Horus. Such interaction is only possible when the cylinders conform to the proportions of the Golden Section, also known as the Golden mean or golden ratio which is connected to the Fibonacci numbers and the golden section in nature, art, geometry, architecture, music and even for calculating pi. The height of Wands of Horus is attuned to the pyramid and the diameter of the Wands is designed to be tuned to the Earth 'Eigen frequency' which is a natural frequency, an inner frequency and a self-frequency. When we delve into ancient advanced knowledge of universe and self we cannot but help stumbling across mathematics, sound and frequencies. This is because the very fabric of existence is universal mathematical code.

But there is a frequency significant to the ancient Egyptians and that is 432 Hertz. Ths can also be found hidden within the star of David.

Frequencies understood by the Egyptians were rediscovered by modern science with the Schuman frequency, also known as the Schumann Resonance Properties

The spherical earth-ionosphere cavity is created by the conductive surface of the earth and the outer boundary of the ionosphere, separated by non-conducting air. Electromagnetic impulses are generated by electrical discharges such as lightning, the main excitation source, and spread laterally into the cavity. Lightning discharges have a "high-frequency component", involving frequencies between 1 kHz and 30 kHz, followed by a "low-frequency component" consisting of waves and frequencies below 2 kHz and gradually increasing amplitude. This produces electromagnetic waves in the very low frequency (VLF) and extremely low frequency (ELF) ranges. ELF waves at 3 Hz to 300 Hz are propagated as more or less strongly attenuated waves in the space between the earth and the ionosphere, which provides a waveguide for the signals. Certain wavelengths circumnavigate the earth with little attenuation due to the fact that standing waves are formed within the cavity, the circumference of which is "approximately equal to the wavelength which an electromagnetic wave with a frequency of about 7.8 Hz would have in free space" (König, 1979, p34). It is the waves of this frequency and its harmonics at 14, 20, 26, 33, 39 and 45 Hz that form Schumann Resonances.

On a global scale the total resonant spectrum is the effect of the global lightning worldwide which is estimated at an average of 100 strokes per second. Since there is a concentration of lightning activity during the afternoon in Southeast Asia, Africa and America there are Schumann Resonance amplitude peaks at 10, 16 and 22 UT (universal time), with activity over America around 22 UT being dominant. There are also +/- 0.5 Hz variations in the centre frequency, caused by a diurnal increase in ionization of the ionosphere as a result of radiation from the sun, having the effect of reducing the height of the ionosphere at 12 local time. Another factor which influences centre frequency is sunspot activity.

During his research another scientist Dr Ludwig came across the ancient Chinese teachings which state that Man needs two environmental signals: the YANG (masculine) signal from above and the YIN (feminine) signal from below. This description fits the relatively strong signal of the Schumann wave surrounding our planet being YANG and the weaker geomagnetic waves coming from below, from within the planet, being the YIN signal. This requires a balance of opposites and the balance of self, which was fully understood in ancient Egypt.

432 Hertz is the Godlike state, a perfect frequency and when we use mathematics we get from this number the formula 4+3+2 = 9, 432 Hertz and Hertz means the amount of oscillations per second. This frequency releases DMT from your pineal gland which makes it easy to go straight into the avatar state. An Avatar is a manifestation of a deity or released soul in bodily form on earth, an incarnate divine teacher. DMT is a Psychedelic serum within the brain taking us into a spiritual mode. Chants at the right frequency help release Dimenthyltryptamine (DMT) which is a hallucinogenic drug that can be produced by the brain especially during REM sleep. The Egyptians used vowel sounding chants

The Ancient Code - A Serpent Fire

to invoke certain reactions to enhance this practice. 432HZ is a perfect balanced tone that helps you to grow metaphysically. The diameter of the moon is precisely 2160 miles which is exactly 432 x 5. The diameter of the sun is 864.000 miles which is 432.000 x 2. The number 432 is also found in the patterns of planet orbits. Pythagoras (570 - 495 BC) was a Greek philosopher, mathematician, astronomer and scientist. He was credited for originating the "music of the spheres" theory which states there are musical intervals (mathematical ratios) found in the distances and sizes of the planets and how they moved around one another. It gave name to the Pythagorean Tuning scale which turns out to produce the A=432 Hz! 432 is encoded into the very workings of the cosmos. Listening to the 432Hz frequency resonates inside our body, releases emotional blockages and expands our consciousness. 432Hz is the 'Miracle Tone' and raises positive vibrations and it is a healing frequency. 432 Hertz is pitching 'A' on the musical scale. A = 432 Hz, known as Verdi's 'A' is an alternative tuning that is mathematically consistent with the universe. Music based on 432Hz transmits beneficial healing energy, because it is a pure tone of maths fundamental connection to nature. Verdi was a composer and it is said that the famous composers tuned their music and symphonies to this tone and frequency also. The letter 'A' is also the Pyramid shape and would resonate with the same tone and frequency. Archaic Egyptian instruments that have been unearthed are largely tuned to A=432Hz. 432Hz unites you with the universal harmony. This tone is closely related to the universe around us, it is the pitch of energy release, chakra tuning, relaxation and meditation and healing. 432 hertz is enlightened consciousness. Ancient Egyptian instruments such as the Sistra or sistrum are tuned to this frequency and its importance can be seen in many carvings and hieroglyphs shown in the Temples of Egypt.

The number 216 is the number of the beast, man and is one octave below 432 hertz. In the bible the number of the beast is 666, but if we make this mathematical equation 6x6x6 we get 216. If we take the Hebrew letters and their numerical value to create geometry they fit into the 216 outline triangle, which again is the Pyramid shape. If the octave of man is 216 then the octave higher is 432, the Egyptians were taking themselves from man to God, 216+216=432.

(The letter 'A' forms the pyramid shape)

Going back to Verdi's 'A' in the Hebrew language the word Aleph as in the first letter of the alphabet, means 'Father' or the head of royalty (king). Aleph has the gemetria of 1, in other words at 1 with God as the material realm, the four sides of the Pyramid, turn into a connection with the ether, the fifth element at the capstone, where we go from man to God-like. The significance of the 'Head of Royalty' is contained in the earlier passage regarding the word Pharaoh meaning 'Great House' which in other words is 'Great Mind'.

342 is a sacred universal number that other cultures have harnessed too. For example at the Buddhist Borobudur Temple in Indonesia there are 432 Statues of Buddha which is an esoteric reference to this number. Even Tibetan singing bowls are set at this frequency. The Lotus flower is significant in these cultures as well as in Egypt where in addition to enlightenment the Egyptians also saw it as the joining of Lower and Upper Egypt due to its intertwining stems.

The Ancient Code - A Serpent Fire

(8 Sided Pyramid)

Many believe that the Great pyramid has 4 sides which is how it appears to the naked eye. However during the summer solstice (solstice meaning sun standing still) there appears to be an indentation that gives us the appearance of 8 sides. This is again harmonic frequencies because with multiple cycles of 8 we get a significant 432. And to put an extra synchronicity or three to this when I was writing the Egyptian section in my book 'The secrets of the Pyramids – A message for Humanity' and speaking about 432 I just happened to look down, for no reason, at the word count and it was 432 at that stage! Then shortly after I got a social media request to like someone's page which was called... you guessed it, 432 Hertz! Later that evening, a few hours after, I was walking down a set of stairs whereby I heard a sound I can only describe as a whoosh inside my head and in a split-second I saw a Pharaoh of Egypt in full Golden Serpent headdress.

We have been left a wonderful advanced knowledge by our ancient ancestors and as the full picture reveals itself piece by piece I sit here in wonderment. The Pyramids represent consciousness and how to reach it. Not only was one of the pyramid shafts facing Orion/Osiris to show us the connection to the Pineal gland (also relevant to the Kings chamber) but also the three main pyramids of Giza are aligned to the constellation of Orion too, to reinforce this message.

Many scholars have correctly identified the advanced mathematics within the pyramids that make up their dimensions and structure but what they have missed are their pinnacle purpose, which are their numerical frequencies of consciousness and how to invoke consciousness. It is true that we can find advanced mathematics within them but they are not simply mathematics which is a fact these scholars have also seemingly missed. These mathematical numbers are there not only for design and structural building diameters but also for the consciousness frequencies of the numbers themselves. For example 3.14159 which is PI. PI vibrates at 528 hertz which is known as the miracle tone restoring consciousness to full potential, and 528 Hertz is a frequency that is central to the musical mathematical matrix of creation. Amazingly within the numerical digits of PI there is encoded the states of the brain within the numerical digits themselves and also the atomic co-ordinates of the human atomic and genetic code. PI is a transcendental number meaning it deals with the spirit realm and gives us quantum immortality.

There are other famous number sequences too such as the Golden mean/ratio and of course the Fibonacci sequence which we are told by the history books was discovered by Leonardo De Pisa in 1202, this is not correct as it was used in the Egyptian pyramids. Nevertheless the Golden ratio and the Fibonacci sequence both have a frequency of 432 hertz which I have already discussed in terms of extreme relevance and also the balance of the third dimension.

THE MUMMY RETURNS:

In Egypt upon the mummification process we have the Canopic Jars (Canopic derives from the South Pole star Canopus which has consciousness raising star frequencies) with body parts placed within and protected by the 4 Sons of Horus: The 4 cardinal points of the compass. The 4 sons of Horus are as follows:

Imsety

Qebehsenuf

Hapy

Duamatef

Mummification was the living spirit of man enclosed within the material form, symbolised by the Mummy case.

Also as previously discussed the Pyramid, directly behind the Sphinx (and therefore shielded/protected by), is the endocrine system that connects us to God, the sphinx is the protector of the Throne of God, the God-mind, our God-like consciousness. Throne of God is also another expression for the Pineal gland. The Atef crown worn by many Egyptian Gods is symbolic of the brain opened out and exposing the component parts of the third eye endocrine system. Atef means 'His might'. God, we are told in the biblical scriptures, is light and our pineal Gland is our inner light, the Amun Ra, the seat of the soul. Its divinity must be protected and this is the message given to us by this symbolic guardian in the desert. The human mind, replicated by the Great Pyramid, in the internal sense is the natural and rational mind where intelligence and wisdom reside, the human mind, the 'Throne of God'. The initiates were protecting the wisdom and the key to divinity for the worthy.

The Egyptians, through and with their magnificent monuments, were showing us the anatomy of the human brain, a gigantic replica of our Endocrine third eye system of consciousness and how to achieve divinity and cosmic consciousness by the balancing of opposites at the apex, indicated by the Golden Pyramid capstone, were duality becomes whole, it becomes one, we have mastered the physical world, with each chakra having first been balanced. This was so large that its importance could be in no doubt. They wanted to show us how much it meant to them and what value it had been placed upon it, a massive statement in the desert. And it isn't only Pyramids, many Churches and Cathedrals are also showing the endocrine system when you overlay a figure of the human head over the floor plans of churches/cathedrals too.

The Halls of Amenti, the ultimate hall of mirrors, is the realm of the great illusion that is only passable by knowledge and wisdom. After passing the Halls of Amenti merger with the Omega Point follows. The Halls of Amenti are the 'Hidden Mind'! Omega is the highest form of consciousness and of course Christ was known as the Alpha and Omega.

We have been left in the most grand and significant way the key and path to enlightenment by an advanced race that knew the secrets of body and universe and its connections. Maybe we can follow them into greatness! Consciousness was everything to the hierarchy of Egyptian society and all that they did was working towards the God-state.

As stated and just as importantly as external sun worship was 'Amun Ra' which means hidden light/sun and although the Pineal gland is seen as the inner light due to its illumination at the point of consciousness awakening there is also another light that is pinnacle. That other light is biophotons and they hold the key to the quality of life in all things and also create the auric field, and when we are unwell we feel 'off colour'. This and other secrets which I will mention soon are encoded within the pyramids. The Great Pyramid (Great also means multi-dimensional, in the case of the Great pyramid it represents the multidimensional mind), is 449 feet high. This was not a random number by chance for this reason. 449 Nanometres is the wavelength of produced biophotons within the neurons of the brain, it is quantum entanglement (the branch of science that deals with how atoms and particles interact together) and is connected to consciousness. And the more light (biophotons) the more consciousness. Biophotons vibrate at 728 hertz which is an advanced frequency of healing and deals with a higher level of consciousness. It is the frequency of cellular cleansing and balancing. Cells and DNA use biophotons to store and communicate information. This inner light/inner sun in combination with the illumination of our pineal gland at the point of enlightenment is the 'Amun Ra' the hidden sun.

This is the eye of Horus hidden in a secret coded way, it is the pineal gland:

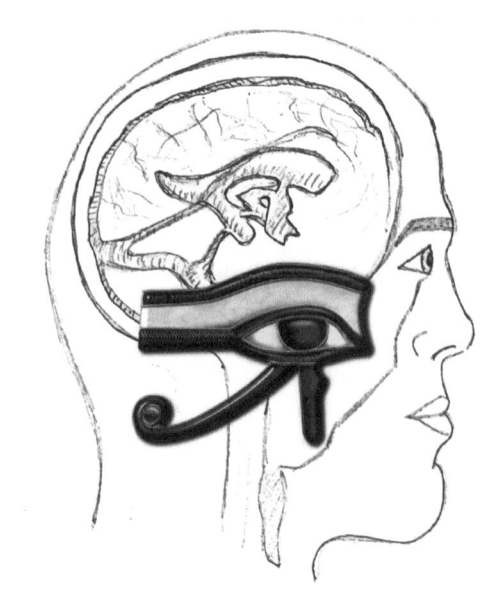

(Pineal Gland / Eye of Horus)

Another secret Egyptian trait was the Kohl, the black eyeliner around their eyes which has caused some speculation as to its meaning. Some say it was medicinal but I can tell you exactly what it represents, The God Osiris who was God of the underworld name means 'Seat or throne of the soul' and Osiris is the Pineal gland which is the throne/seat of the soul. He is also known as the God of the staircase which is referring to the spine which leads to the head and the temple of enlightenment. The colour, or one of the colours, associated with Osiris is black and the eye liner is representing Osiris as the third eye. And this is why we see the likes of these pieces of Egyptian art:

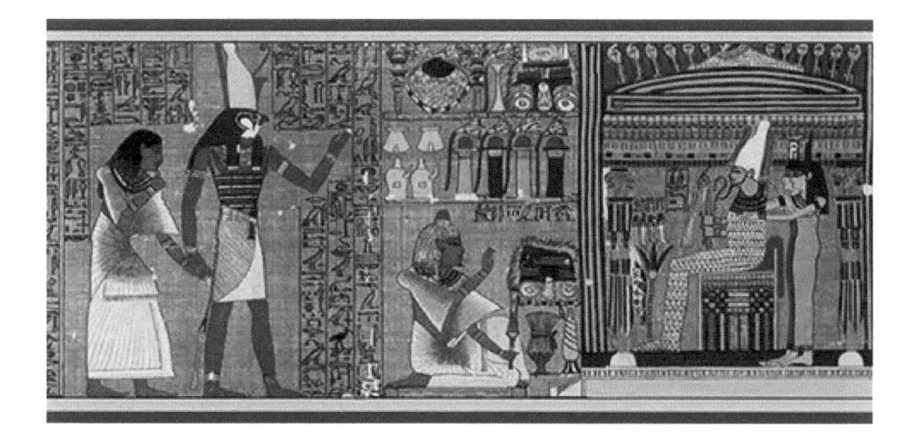

(This is the scene described above with Osiris (Pineal gland) judging the soul from the throne (throne means seat) of the soul, we of course use our pineal gland to see beyond this third dimensional world of ours)

The Great Pyramid is located in Giza and when we use a compass map of all 4 cardinal points and include the coordinates such as NW, SW, SE, NE, in between we get the union jack shape and the red and white colours are Upper and Lower Egypt, and blue is Royalty.

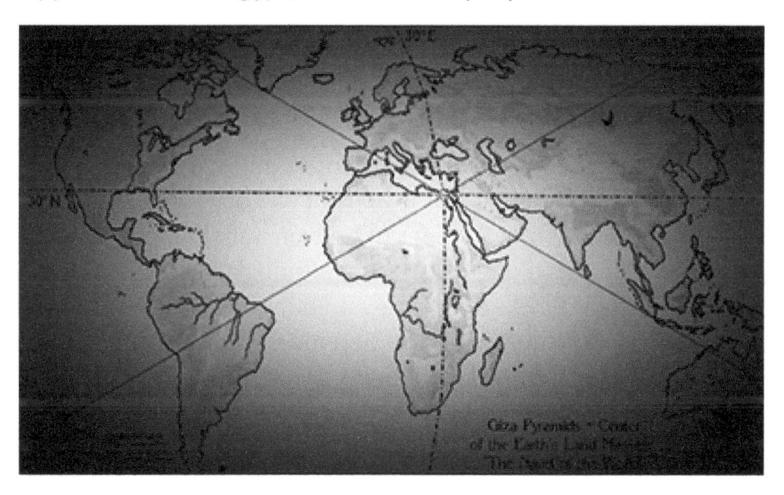

(Centre of cardinal lines indicate location of Giza in Egypt)

The 4 cardinal points that the Great Pyramid is locked into means this:

North is Wisdom and Logic

East is enlightenment and Illumination

South is emotions

West is introspection which means the examination of your own mental processes.

All of these must be balanced as one. So there you have it, the mystery solved. The Great pyramid is the human brain's consciousness functions, the mathematics of the pyramids are numeric consciousness frequencies and balance is the way of attaining Christ consciousness. We are being told in the most wondrous of ways and all we need do is listen and hear!

There are many monuments all around the world that are aligned to the constellation of Orion and this is for the exact same reason, consciousness and its connection to the Pineal gland. This proves that these ancient cultures were tapping into the same knowledge base. And here are just a few examples of note:

Teotihuacán

Located in the highlands of central Mexico, 35 miles northeast of present day Mexico City lays the ruins of the ancient city of Teotihuacán, another marvel of the ancient world with ties to star constellations. Archaeologists and scholars debate the age of the site, although it is generally agreed upon that the city flourished for at least 500 years before it completely collapsed by the 7th century of the Common Era. The city was one of the largest in the world at its peak, with an approximate population of 150,000-200,000 people. Despite the fact that the city predated the Aztecs by several centuries, they called it Teotihuacán, meaning the "Place of the Gods", as they believed that it was the place where the current world was created. Like many sacred sites from the ancient world, the observatories, pyramids, and structures at Teotihuacán are constructed mirroring celestial alignments. The complex at Teotihuacán contains three pyramids, two larger and one smaller, boasting a similarity to the layout of the pyramids at Giza and forming another correlation to the belt of Orion. The Pyramid of the Sun is said to be aligned with the Pleiades, another constellation of great importance in myth and lore that is often connected to the constellation of Orion.

Sacred Alignment of the Hopi

The Hopi are a Native American tribe whose cosmology, monuments, and landscape have a deep connection with the constellation of Orion. For many generations, they built and abandoned villages before settling on an area comprised of three mesas in the north eastern part of Arizona, where they have been for over a thousand years.

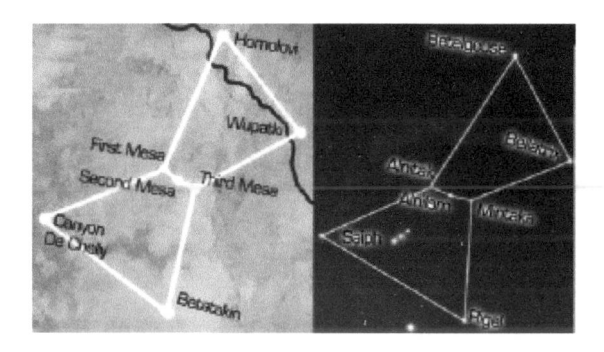

(Constellation of Orion, Orion's Belt)

The natural structure of the three mesas mirrors are the three stars in the belt of Orion, and it is said that this is why the Hopi chose to settle in this location. They believe this place to be the centre of their universe, where they can make contact with the gods. Furthermore, when connected to other Hopi monuments and landmarks around the southwest, the collective sites are said to map the entire constellation of Orion.

Around 500 miles south of Cairo, we will find on a desolate plain in the eastern region of the Sahara Desert the mysterious archaeological site known as Nabta Playa. Discovered by a team of scientists in 1974, researchers believe the stones scattered here were once part of a vast ritual centre for an ancient civilization that thrived from 6400 to 3400 B.C., just before the rise of the Egyptians. Nabta Playa is different it wasn't a settlement. One of the centre pieces is a circle that has been called the "mini Stonehenge of the desert." For more than three decades, this circular stone structure and its intricate alignment to the stars of the Orion constellation have baffled archaeologists. The builders of Nabta Playa seem to be aware of a level of physics and understandings of mathematics that allowed them to build these structures in relation to the Orion constellation. There are of course many more examples of Orion's correlation with ancient monuments.

Egypt was and is a fascinating land. It also gave rise to what we know of today as holistic alternative health created by Imhotep who was known as the 'Prince of peace' although this form of medication has not been attributed to Egypt. Holistic is characterized by the belief that the parts of something are intimately interconnected and explicable only by reference to the whole. In medical terms it is characterized by the treatment of the whole person, taking into account mental and social factors, rather than just the symptoms of a disease.

I am pleased that its depth and its secrets have reached you.

The 'Ancient Code' that I have deciphered is enlightened consciousness...

14

Stonehenge: The Cyclopean Ritual

Stonehenge: The Cyclopean Ritual

(Me visiting Stonehenge, Wiltshire, 2008)

Modern man believes that he has the most updated knowledge of our existence and we are supposedly now at the pinnacle of human development and in its most current year and time. We regard all that has gone before us, especially our ancient past occupied by our ancient ancestors, as being primitive and basic. Or at least that is what we're told publically. We are told that the likes of the Pyramids of Egypt were built by Hebrew slaves who transported large and heavy stones for miles and erected them over 400 feet high in the desert using only the most basic of tools. We are told that ancient man had basic knowledge and used stones to create cosmic calendars to map out the year, which is partly true, as the planets influence us and our chakra system with each planet ruling a certain chakra and therefore it was important to know where a particular planet is/was in the sky to enhance that chakra balancing hence star maps, but it goes much deeper. And as I have eluded to in some of my previous books such as 'The Secrets of the Pyramids – A message for Humanity' their knowledge is far more advanced than we give them credit for, in fact they had more knowledge of the workings of the human body, its energy systems and its self than we do today.

They knew how to extract information from their own DNA and they knew how to advance their own physical vessels. They understood Earth's meridians and used them to create their own God-state consciousness. They were more in tune with nature and knew how to connect to it to get their higher levels of themselves activated. They were much more connected to their world than we are today and they were not disconnected by fancy electrical devices of the 21st century that actually takes us away from our true essence. Devices that are partly mechanical advancement and partly a deliberate intervention that keeps us from our true potential, by constant distraction and health concerning omissions. I have written extensively about other cultures such as the Egyptians and I have also touched upon others such as the Sumerians, the Greeks and the Mayans.

These cultures talk about the same subject and they have left us a transcript within their famous monuments and mythical Gods and Goddesses. That message is about our true self, our true essence and how to achieve the God-state, the higher mind! And despite popular belief that these cultures were a separate entity they were not, they were deeply connected and had the same knowledge base which means that they had communications of some kind between themselves or even with a higher aspect overseeing everything and co-ordinating from a greater panoramic viewpoint. This can be proven beyond any doubt by mathematics and other means. All the famous monuments of Earth and even further afield on planet Mars are connected by mathematical co-ordinates that give the exact locations of each other that are contained within their diameters and proportions. This is impossible without co-ordination of the greatest heights. The universe is a mathematic design and all things large and small on Earth and in the cosmos follow a mathematical code. Even the foetus grows to a mathematical grid. From the nautilus shell of the snail to the large plasma pinch effect of spiral galaxies, all are encoded. Maths is a universal language that we are only touching the surface of even in our modern era. But having found the secret teachings and messages left for us and contained within the Pyramids of Egypt and within the famous

Stonehenge: The Cyclopean Ritual

'Sumerian Scrolls' deciphered by the late author Zecharia Sitchen, which were a literal translation and not correct, to the real identity of the characters of the bible such as Jesus Christ, Mary Magdalene, Moses and Noah, Mary and Joseph, I have now deciphered the secret coded and messages within another world famous monument namely Stonehenge using the same blueprint.

My wife and I visited Stonehenge in 2009 and heard the many versions of their purpose and their builders. From the Druids, who I will go into further in a little while, to Merlin and also a race of giants, who dropped the stones used to build the Stonehenge, during a transit between two places across Salisbury Plain. But despite the efforts of the mainstream there seemed to me, as always, a greater purpose and a deeper mystery and I have discovered that there indeed is. So in fine tradition of my research and work please join me for some revelations.

Salisbury Plain is a chalk plateau in the south western part of central southern England covering 300 square miles (780 km2). It is part of a system of chalk down lands throughout eastern and southern England formed by the rocks of the Chalk Group and largely lies within the county of Wiltshire, but also stretching into Berkshire and Hampshire. The plain is famous for its rich archaeology, including Stonehenge, one of England's best known landmarks. Largely as a result of the establishment of the Defence Training Estate Salisbury Plain (DTE SP), the plain is sparsely populated and is the largest remaining area of calcareous grassland in north-west Europe. Additionally the plain has arable land, and a few small areas of beech trees and coniferous woodland. Its highest point is Easton Hill. Salisbury Plain is famous for its history and archaeology. In the Neolithic period Stone Age man began to settle on the plain, most likely centred around the causeway enclosure of Robin Hood's Ball. Large long barrows like White Barrow and other earthworks were built across the plain. By 2500 BC areas around Durrington Walls and Stonehenge had become a focus for building, and the southern part of the plain continued to be settled into the Bronze Age. Around 600 BC Iron Age Hill forts came to be constructed around the boundaries of the plain, including Scratchbury Camp and Battlesbury Camp to the south west, Bratton Camp to the North West, Casterley Camp to the north, Yarnbury and Vespasian's Camp to the south, and Sidbury Hill to the east. Roman roads are visible features, probably serving a settlement near Old Sarum. Villas are sparse, however, and Anglo-Saxon place names suggest that the plain was mostly a grain-producing imperial estate. In the 6th century Anglo-Saxon incomers built planned settlements in the valleys surrounded by strip lynchets, with the downland left as sheep pasture. To the south is the city of Salisbury, whose 13th and 14th century cathedral is famous for having the tallest spire in the country, and the building was, for many centuries, the tallest building in Britain. The cathedral is evidence of the prosperity the wool and cloth trade brought to the area. In the mid-19th century the wool and cloth industry began to decline, leading to a decline in the population and change in land use from sheep farming to agriculture and military use. Wiltshire became one of the poorest counties in England during this period of decline. There are a number of chalk carvings on the plain, of which the most famous is the Westbury White Horse. The Kennet and Avon Canal was constructed to the north of the plain, through the Vale of Pewsey.

The theme in all the mainstream versions of ancient history is always one common theme, they always miss the point, and they always miss the deeper meanings and explanations. In order to understand what we are being told by our ancestors you first need to understand the minds of their architects, you must first know what they knew. And you must understand their desire to advance their physical vessels to one of cosmic metaphysical proportions of their true and God-like potential. That was their goal and their ultimate aim as you will see in this chapter.

These are the main components of the Stonehenge and other ancient principles:

CONSCIOUSNESS:

Consciousness is the state or quality of awareness, or, of being aware of an external object or something within oneself. It has been defined variously in terms of sentience, awareness, subjectivity, the ability to experience or to feel, wakefulness, having a sense of selfhood or soul, the fact that there is something "that it is like" to "have" or "be" it, and the executive control system of the mind, or the state or quality of awareness, or, of being aware of an external object or something within oneself. In contemporary philosophy its definition is often hinted at via the logical possibility of its absence, the philosophical zombie, which is defined as a being whose behaviour and function are identical to one's own yet there is "no-one in there" experiencing it. Despite the difficulty in definition, many philosophers believe that there is a broadly shared underlying intuition about what consciousness is.

CHAKRA'S:

The 7 Life Force Energy Centres: "Chakra" is a Sanskrit word literally meaning "wheel." These centres were named as such because of the circular shape to the spinning energy centres which exist in our subtle etheric body, the non-material energetic counterpart to our physical body. There are seven main chakras and they are located along the spine extending out the front and back of the body. Each chakra has a number of specific qualities that correspond to the refinement of energy from the base-level material-self-identity, located at the first chakras, up to the higher vibration spirit-level awareness of being at our crown.

These energetic centres represent our highest level of integration split, prism like, into a spectrum of colours. Our opportunity in studying them is to learn how to master each chakra's essence and unite them all into a unified field of brilliance. As such, we re-unite our disparate parts into a radian light of full self-awareness. The chakras are formed at the junction of three connected energy shafts that ascend the spine, one on each side of the central channel, the Shushumna. Chakras both take up and collect Prana (life force energy also called Mana) and transform and pass on energy. Our material bodies could not exist without them for they serve as gateways for the flow of energy and life into our physical bodies. Each chakra is associated with a certain part of the body and a certain organ which it provides with the energy it needs to function. Additionally, just as every organ in the human body has its equivalent on the mental and spiritual level, so too every chakra corresponds to a specific aspect of human behaviour and development. Our circular spirals of energy differ in size and activity from person to person. They vibrate at different levels relative to the awareness of the individual and their ability to integrate the characteristics of each into their life. The lower chakras are associated with fundamental emotions and needs, for the energy here vibrates at a lower frequency and is therefore denser in nature. The finer energies of the upper chakras correspond to our higher mental and spiritual aspirations and faculties. The openness and flow of energy through our chakras determines our state of health and balance. Knowledge of our more subtle energy system empowers us to maintain balance and harmony on the physical, mental and spiritual level. All meditation and yoga systems seek to balance out the energy of the chakras by purifying the lower energies and guiding them upwards. Through the use of grounding, creating "internal space," and living consciously with an awareness of how we acquire and spend our energy we become capable of balancing our life force with our mental, physical and spiritual selves.

In order for us to become fully self-realised and in harmony with our physical and spiritual nature our denser lower energies need to be harmonized with the lighter energies of the upper centres. Each centre has an integral function in creating our energetic balance. It is through the study of our energetic and physical being that we can create health, emotional stability and spiritual bliss.

KUNDALINI SYSTEM:

The Serpent Power Within: Kundalini (Sanskrit:" coiled one"), in the concept of Dharma, refers to a form of primal energy (or shakti) said to be located at the base of the spine. Different spiritual traditions teach methods of "awakening" kundalini for the purpose of reaching spiritual enlightenment and a range of supernormal powers. It is a white liquid fire that causes either a gradual or sudden change in the volume or quality of bioenergy which is renewable energy produced by living organisms. Liquid fire is a composition of chemicals and ths then goes into the scientific branch of chemistry which is the science of matter, atoms and molecules. It just so happens that the word chemistry, as with alchemy derives from Khem which is another name for Egypt. The colour white is the colour of balance, like the serpent that I saw at my feet.

Writer Joseph Campbell describes the concept of Kundalini as "the figure of a coiled female serpent—a serpent goddess not of "gross" but of "subtle" substance - which is to be thought of as residing in a torpid, slumbering state in a subtle centre, the first of the seven, near the base of the spine: the aim of the yoga then being to rouse this serpent, lift her head, and bring her up a subtle nerve or channel of the spine to the so-called "thousand-petaled lotus" (Sahasrara) at the crown of the head. She, rising from the lowest to the highest lotus centre, will pass through and wake the five between, and with each waking the psychology and personality of the practitioner will be altogether and fundamentally transformed.

Kundalini awakening is said to result from deep meditation, and consequently enlightenment and bliss. However, as each individual is unique, Kundalini awakenings can happen through a variety of methods not limited to deep meditation. This awakening involves the Kundalini physically moving up the central channel to reach within the Sahasrara Chakra at the top of the head. Many systems of yoga focus on awakening Kundalini through meditation, pranayama breathing, the practice of asana and chanting of mantras. In physical terms, the Kundalini experience is frequently reported to be a feeling of electric current running along the spine. Numerous accounts describe the experience of Kundalini awakening. When awakened, Kundalini is said to rise up from the muladhara chakra through the central nadi (called sushumna) inside or alongside the spine and reaching the top of the head. The progress of Kundalini through the different chakras leads to different levels of awakening and mystical experience, until Kundalini finally reaches the top of the head, Sahasrara or crown chakra, producing an extremely profound transformation of consciousness. Energy is said to accumulate in the muladhara and the yogi seeks to send it up to the brain, transforming it into 'Ojas', the highest form of energy.

We have a mystical system within us that the ancients were fully aware of and knew how to utilise to better themselves. They understood the meridians of both Earth and the body and how they were completely connected. They understood the need to balance such systems in order to reach the heights of higher self. They knew that in order to do this their body had to be balanced and prepared. It was the higher state of human.

The Endocrine System: Meaning 'secretion within' and secretion gives us the word secret...

At the top of our chakra system we have the endocrine system, endocrine means 'Secretion within' and secretion gives us the word secret. And it is a secret that our awakening is triggered by these glands. They are part of a quadrant system of consciousness, the Pineal Gland, the Pituitary Gland and the Thalamus, we also have an overseer that is not a chakra but is the Cerebellum (meaning 'Little Brain'). The endocrine system is made up of glands that produce and secrete hormones, chemical substances produced in the body that regulate the activity of cells or organs. These hormones regulate the body's growth, metabolism (the physical and chemical processes of the body), and sexual development and function. The hormones are released into the bloodstream and may affect one or several organs throughout the body. Hormones are chemical messengers created by the body. They transfer information from one set of cells to another to coordinate the functions of different parts of the body. The major glands of the endocrine system are the hypothalamus, pituitary, thyroid, parathyroids, adrenals, pineal body, and the reproductive organs (ovaries and testes).

The pancreas is also a part of this system, it has a role in hormone production as well as in digestion.

The endocrine system is regulated by feedback in much the same way that a thermostat regulates the temperature in a room. For the hormones that are regulated by the pituitary gland, a signal is sent from the hypothalamus to the pituitary gland in the form of a "releasing hormone," which stimulates the pituitary to secrete a "stimulating hormone" into the circulation. The stimulating hormone then signals the target gland to secrete its hormone. As the level of this hormone rises in the circulation, the hypothalamus and the pituitary gland shut down secretion of the releasing hormone and the stimulating hormone, which in turn slows the secretion by the target gland. This system results in stable blood concentrations of the hormones that are regulated by the pituitary gland. When balanced they give rise to cosmic transcendence and higher consciousness awakening.

The Druids have long been associated with Stonehenge and held initiation ceremonies for new members at the site itself under the guise of the 'Ancient and Archaeological Order of Druids' (AAOD) of which the likes of War time British Prime Minister Winston Churchill was a member. They also attend Stonehenge to commemorate the 'Summer Solstice' even today. There have been many splinter groups under different names such as the 'Druid Order' or the 'Ancient Druid Order' and also "The British Circle of the Universal Bond" and "An Druidh Uileach Braithreachas" meaning "The Universal Druid Brotherhood". I at one point could not take my gaze off solitary Oak trees in fields and when I looked into the Druids I discovered that the word Dru-id means Oak knowledge!

The Druids used the wood from the holly tree for their magic wands and this in the modern day is the magic of Hollywood! Hollywood has an astrological theme with its stars and 'A' listers which are common stars seen by the naked eye. But who were they? The Druids were connected to the ancient mystery schools of Egypt and were known as the 'Serpent Priests' who wore the 'Hoshen' breastplate on their chests. This is symbolised by the portcullis that can be seen on the seating of the House of Commons in British Parliament and on some British monetary coins. They were called the Djedhi (Jedi in Starwars) and knew many secrets of life and existence. They came to the British Isles from Egypt armed with such esoteric knowledge. They were connected to nature and its secrets and when I talk about nature that also extends to the cosmos which are both connected. We see Druids in Stonehenge dressed in robes and traditional attire on our TV screens every Solstice and some may scoff at the ritual, some of them are simply playing along for the ride, but there are those who truly know that they are part of a linear line of a culture who understood the esoteric meaning of human existence and its true place in amongst all things.

STONEHENGE – THE MYSTERY REVEALED

I now take you back to the beginning of the chapter and to the chakra system of enlightenment, which is not only pinnacle in ancient Egypt, Sumer, Babylon, Greece and others but also in the monoliths of Stonehenge. All have the same purpose and workings of balance and synergy. The whole area of this region which also contains Stonehenge itself was believed to have spanned over several miles. Originally 700 stones may have been present in various locations within that region which looks different today from what it did then. The number 700 is very apt as it represents the evolution of the microcosm, the seven principles of the man. It is the symbol of the Resurrection as an image of the Phoenix, this mythological bird that once burnt and reappeared out of its own ashes. In Greek, the numerical value of Phoenix, FOINIX, gives us the number 700 = 500+70+10+50+10+60. The Numerical value of words and letters is known as Gemetria. The well- known adage the 'Phoenix from the flames' is really referring to Kundalini activation as it travels to the third eye and sets it alight with its energy of fire.

According to the ancient Chinese, a vital energy circulates through the body on the specific paths called meridians. This vital energy makes surface on the skin with more than 700 different points. It is on the balancing of this vital energy of the body.

Tall stones have seven 'bands' of energy (range of energy). While the Earth Kundalini travels from the middle of the Earth up through the perineum and straight through the middle of the body and out the top of the head the Body Kundalini begins at the base of the spine and travels up the spine and out the top of the head. This requires preparation and balance and purity of the body in order to facilitate such a transition. The seven bands equate to our chakras (Energetic chakra bands) and our ancient ancestors utilized a powerful circular Earth energy pattern known as a Primary Halo. It is highly magnetic and invariably consists of three concentric circles of energy and standing stones and mounds were sited upon them. This is the reason why the ancients chose a circular design for their stone circles and mounds and sacred sites mark their location within the esoteric landscape. Concentric means of or denoting circles, arcs, or other shapes which share the same centre, the larger often completely surrounding the smaller.

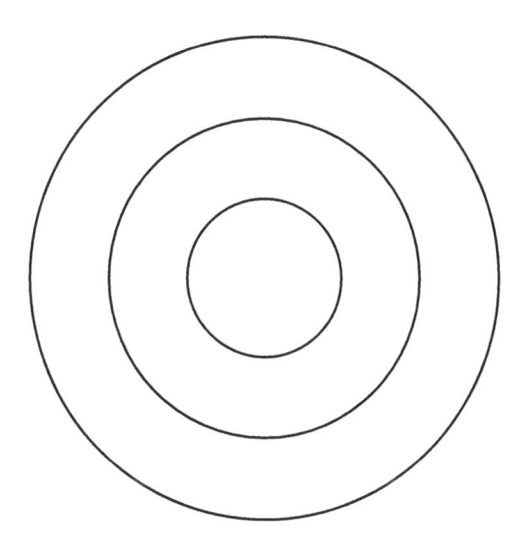

(Concentric Circle)

Blue stones were originally formed into an oval shape (the shape of our pituitary gland). But later the Bluestones were arranged in a circle between the two rings of sarsens and in an oval at the centre of the inner ring. Constructing Europe's unusual Megalithic and Cyclopean architecture was based on a mysterious "technique" which involved tapping the strength of the "god within" by awakening the "Cyclopean" or Third Eye. Preseli Bluestone (originally outer circle) activates the Soma Chakra, located at the hairline above the third eye. This is a higher resonance of the third eye, when activated the soma chakra opens metaphysical awareness and visionary ability. It also has to do with perception of the cycles of time and awareness and the workings of synchronicity. When this chakra is functioning well it gives you the mental clarity necessary to achieve en-lighten-ment and promotes lucid dreaming. It unites the pituitary gland that governs physical function with the pineal gland, transcendent spiritual awareness. Preseli Bluestone helps you connect to Earth energies and the wisdom of the Celtic Druidic peoples. Bluestone assists you to move beyond time to access the past or future and this is the reason it was chosen. A megalith should be regarded as a semiconductor 'macrochip' (large electronics- opposite of microchip) which has the capacity to store and transmit energy. They are energy beams that connect all stone circles across the landscape, using Earth energy. Sited upon Earth energy geometries they absorb and transmit energy (Energy grids networks). They are Geodetic-megalithic energy of which there are several in any stone circle. They generate geodetic energies. The rising of Earth's Kundalini (Serpent of Light) that happens within and through us connects with the 'Unity Consciousness Grid'.

To support our greatest well-being, and to make possible our evolution and spiritual awakening, we must allow ourselves (and our brainwave patterns) to breath in concert with mother Earth and with her natural cycles moment-to-moment. The Earth is a spherical receiver of cosmic energy (evolutionary intelligence) which directs our biological process and spiritual evolutionary unfoldment.

The Earth reradiates the cosmic information it receives from its core outward in complex longwave signals. We receive these signals via our spinal columns and cranial structures (a vertical antenna system). The cranial cavity, the capstone to this antenna captures this information and refocuses it to the pineal gland, a neuro-endocrine transducer in the centre of the brain, where it is then transmitted (via the hypothalamus) as signals that direct the pituitary gland, the master control centre of the Brain. These signals are further distributed via the rest of the neurological system. In planetary harmonics the frequency of Venus activates the pineal gland and from the Egyptian chapter you will know that it has a consciousness raising frequency. PI is also pinnacle in consciousness again having discussed this in the chapter about the Pyramids. All afterlife realms exist as afterlife dimensions inhabiting the same space just at different frequencies or vibrations. Tracking Venus also gave rise to the megalithic Yard (MY), a distance of 2.72 metres also known as 'Eulers number' which is a fraction short of PI. Venus was important to the builders of Stonehenge and also in modern day society as it represents the Pentagram, taking a pentagram shaped orbit and is therefore connected to the number 5, the fifth element, the ether and not forgetting its hertz consciousness raising frequencies too, vibrating at 442 hertz. This is the real reason for Stonehenge, it was a cosmic power station to awaken the consciousness of the individuals who were present, taking them to greater places using the energy and power of Earth transmitted through themselves as an antennae.

So there you have it, Stonehenge was an energy grid used to harness Earth's serpent Kundalini energy and in turn to transmute their own chakra system into cosmic consciousness, the God-Head or God-state.

This is an ancient principle of enlightenment used by all the famous cultures that I have previously mentioned in this book. It is a linear channel of cosmic energy from the core of Earth through the human body and into the ether during our Kundalini awakening. This has been practised extensively throughout our ancient ancestral history and is still today by the initiates of certain organisations who have retained this in-depth knowledge themselves purely for themselves. The general populous will never know this knowledge as they are falsely taught about their reality which is created for them by the same groups of initiates and 'Brotherhoods'. The simple fact is we do not know about our self, we do not even consider our capabilities and we are never accurately taught about these things. Until we understand ourselves we can never reach our true potential and we can never access our rightful inheritance namely knowledge. We must understand that we are multi-faceted and multi-dimensional and we are the make- up of the stars, planets and the cosmos.

There is no such thing as scarcity, everything exists in abundance and there is no need to fight and argue over our harsh and low materialistic percentage because of such abundance, but living in this fourth Reich system we are made to suffer.

There is also another intriguing display of intergalactic mathematics (mathematics = Mathema = to know) discovered by mathematician Carl Munck which acts as a pyramid matrix system and a universal satellite navigation system. This set of numerical sequences has a hidden code that reveals the location of other monuments of both Earth and the planet Mars encoded within the diameters of that particular monument. And this is how it works. Stonehenge in Wiltshire, UK, is a 360 degree circle that has 60 outer stones and 15 centre blocks. When we use the mathematical formula 360x60 it equals 21,600 which is a multiple of 51 degrees divided by 10 divided by 42.35 (51 degrees + 10 minutes 42.35 seconds) which is the exact location of Stonehenge. 2160 is also in years the age of the zodiac sign transition, each sign rules for that period of time before the next sign takes over. Stonehenge is 288 feet across which when multiplied by PI and multiplied by 15 (centre block number) divided by the square root 15 we get 52,562 which is the exact grid longitude of Stonehenge. 52,562 divided by 360 PI = a square root of 2160. Square root 2160 divided by 2 PI is the grid reference of the 3 smaller pyramids in Egypt which are adjacent to the Great pyramid and the two other larger pyramids, which equals the square root 2.71 which is the megalithic yard, 2.72 which is also known as 'Euler's number.

360 divided by the megalithic yard squared equals the radius of the Great pyramid itself. When we use the 3 dimensional formation of the Great pyramid using double PI we get 9929,184896 which is the encoded grid latitude of the pyramid of the Cydonian city on planet Mars. And in addition to this the famous face on Mars has a grid latitude of 4523,893421 which when divided by the square root 2160 equals 97,3386882 which is the diameter of Stonehenge. That is also only 1 mile difference to the diameter of the Moon which is 2159 miles.

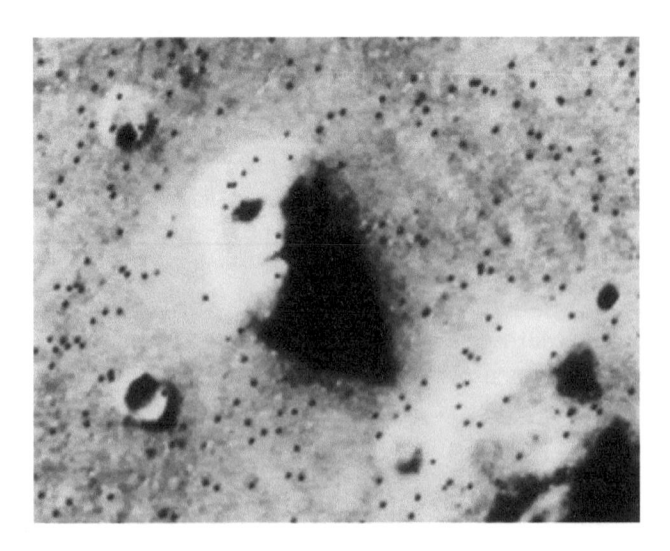

(Face on Mars – Geometrically proven to have been a deliberate design)

Even more evidence of intergalactic communication of the highest mathematical levels is the fact that the Cydonian city on Mars is an exact map overlay of Avebury in Wiltshire, which is the region of Stonehenge.

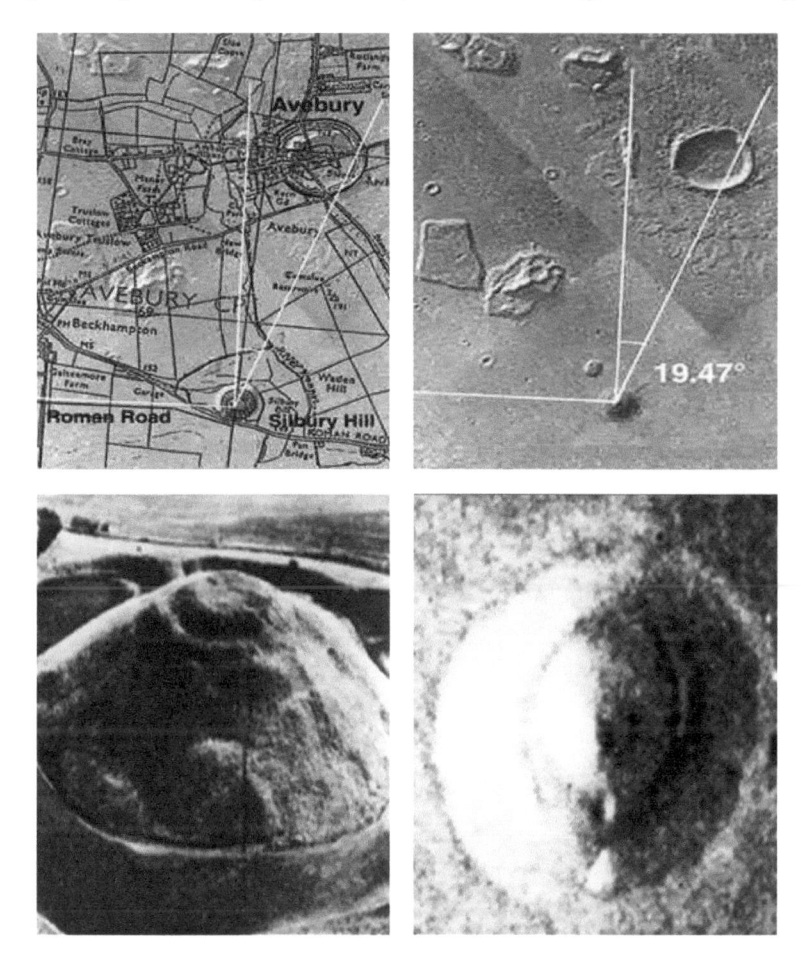

(Top left & right - Avebury & Cydonian City. Bottom left & right - Silbury Hill, Wiltshire & Altar of witness on Mars)

This correlation between encoded mathematical coordinates also extends to other pyramids and sacred monuments and locations too such as in Mexico and elsewhere around the globe. This is beyond ordinary, there is some supernatural panoramic coordination going on at the highest mathematical levels and proves an intergalactic connection beyond doubt. It is a secret code of numbers there to guide others to certain locations between the two planets and that blows the mind. I think we need to re-visit our beliefs and our thinking processes because there is more to our existence than we are being told, so ask yourself, why that is? We are all and we are everything and we have access to everything. We have access to the codes that will transcend us to the 'Great Beyond' and back again should we wish.

15

King Arthur: The Great Bear

Childhood imagination is a wonderful trait seemingly lost at adulthood. The many stories that take our minds on a mental vacation that then seep deep into our hearts for a short time until they become the detached adult memory of fondness. One such story and legend is King Arthur and his round table, the focus of the movie screen and story books but just who was this legendary king that many believe will return one day. But as I always do, I like to decipher hidden ancient codes and discover their true and original meanings and I have done just that in the case of King Arthur, as I have done with the Pyramids of Egypt, Stonehenge, the Sumerian scrolls, the Pirates & treasure stories and the true identities of Biblical characters amongst others. So let's look at the Arthur story in brief and dissect the best known parts piece by piece.

To find the origin of this legend we need look no further than the night sky and its constellations and again that inner aspect of ourselves and the communion of both.

Avalon, the place of residence of King Arthur, derives from the word Avaloch meaning the place of apples and an apple is symbolic of an Allegory which is a story with a hidden meaning (as in the Garden of Eden story). The name Arthur derives from Artos meaning Bear in the Celtic language. The story has Druid connections too and the Druids were the Egyptian mystery school 'Serpent Priests' which is also relevant on a personal level to myself. In the sky above us at certain times of the year we can see the constellation the 'Great Bear' from where we also get the constellation the 'Plough'. The plough is part of Ursa Major forming the Great Bear. A Bear is symbolic in spirituality of Introspection which is the examination of one's own conscious thoughts and knowledge which is relevant in a moment when I talk about the Sword and Stone.

The famous 'Round Table' has been described as the circle in the sky marked by the rotation of the constellation of the Plough around the Pole Star (Polaris, the North Star).

(The Round Table)

This has also been attributed to the Swastika shape too which was originally a Hindu emblem and not what it is associated with now. Swastika means 'of the good'.

Merlin is also a part of the constellation the Plough, the 3 stars in the Ploughs handle are known as the 'Wizards March' and Merlin was Arthur's wizard. Arthur's surname was 'Pendragon' and Pendragon means 'Dragon Master' and Ursa Major is close to the constellation Draco which means Dragon, therefore he is the master of Draco the dragon. The word 'Master' derives from 'Measurer of stars' which has an obvious astronomical connection.

The Lady of the Lake, which also has Druid tradition in the form of Coventina, the Celtic triple goddess of wells and springs, gave Arthur the magical sword Excalibur, thereby making him king and received it again at his death (the famous arm emerging from the water of the lake), symbolising the birth/death cycle which as we saw in the Christ chapter can also be taken to mean the end of Earthly inner consciousness to the transition to outer consciousness (higher consciousness). The sword is symbolic of 'Impenetrable knowledge' and the word 'Excalibur' derives from 'Ex-Calce-Libre' or 'Ex-Calce- Liberatus' meaning 'liberated from the stone'. The stone is the 'Foundation Stone' which is a name for our Pineal Gland associated with knowledge and other worlds. In other words only the chosen few, in this case only King Arthur, can remove the sword, can access this sacred and secret knowledge (the word secret deriving from Secretion, which is the white and brown secretion of the Pineal gland, in biblical terms the land of milk and honey).

The most famous knight of King Arthur legend was Lancelot and one of the meanings of the name Lancelot is God-Like and this whole awakening process takes us to our God-like state, the Egyptian God-head. The Pineal gland is the face of God and with its awakening through Kundalini activation it reconnects us to the ether, the God/father energy which is the consistent theme of all of our ancient cultures.

Even the Norse legend of Odin who sacrificed one eye at the well in return for knowledge is symbolic of the third eye (Pineal gland). Odin (pronounced "OH-din", Old Norse Óðinn, Old English and Old Saxon Woden, Old High German Wuotan, Wotan, or Wodan, Proto-Germanic Woðanaz meaning "Master of Ecstasy" and ecstasy means a trance-like state, originally one involving an experience of mystic self-transcendence, namely enlightenment.

And in Greek myth the Gods of Olympus are really our own god like self that needs to be acknowledged and conversed with in order to maintain it.

The theme is yet again is consciousness and enlightenment and how to achieve it. But as with all the other cryptic stories of enlightenment there is a message hidden within that only the chosen can access it or enjoy its fruits.

Let us now turn that tide.

16

Santa Claus: The Holy Colostrum

The imagination of children the world over is now focused upon one date, the 25th December, when they will be visited by Santa. They've waited all year for this time and the excitement can now be felt globally. As adults we of course know that Santa Claus is a fictional person, or at least we now should (sorry if that came as a bit of a shock to you). But what is he really? Santa Claus is second only in fame to Jesus who himself was not a real person.

As with the real messages of biblical characters and as with ancient cultural enlightenment at the top of society's knowledge base, Santa is no different, he is an aspect of the human brain called the Claustrum. But before I go into the anatomical Santa Claus here's what the mainstream has to say about him in several versions of the character himself.

The story of Santa Claus begins with Nicholas, who was born during the third century in the village of Patara. At the time the area was Greek and is now on the southern coast of Turkey. His wealthy parents, who raised him to be a devout Christian, died in an epidemic while Nicholas was still young. Obeying Jesus' words to "sell what you own and give the money to the poor," (ironic as the Church is one of the richest institutions), Nicholas used his whole inheritance to assist the needy, the sick, and the suffering. He dedicated his life to serving God and was made Bishop of Myra while still a young man. Bishop Nicholas became known throughout the land for his generosity to those in need, his love for children, and his concern for sailors and ships. Under the Roman Emperor Diocletian, who ruthlessly persecuted Christians, Bishop Nicholas suffered for his faith, was exiled and imprisoned. The prisons were so full of bishops, priests, and deacons, there was no room for the real criminals—murderers, thieves and robbers. After his release, Nicholas attended the Council of Nicaea in AD 325.

He died December 6, AD 343 in Myra and was buried in his cathedral church, where a unique relic, called manna, formed in his grave. This liquid substance, (chemical energy processed from sunlight) said to have healing powers, fostered the growth of devotion to Nicholas. The anniversary of his death became a day of celebration, St. Nicholas Day, December 6th (December 19 on the Julian calendar).

Through the centuries many stories and legends have been told of

St. Nicholas' life and deeds. These accounts help us understand his extraordinary character and why he is so beloved and revered as one story tells of a poor man with three daughters. In those days a young woman's father had to offer prospective husbands something of value—a dowry. The larger the dowry the better the chance that a young woman would find a good husband. Without a dowry, a woman was unlikely to marry. This poor man's daughters, without dowries, were therefore destined to be sold into slavery. Mysteriously, on three different occasions, a bag of gold appeared in their home-providing the needed dowries. The bags of gold, tossed through an open window, are said to have landed in stockings or shoes left before the fire to dry. This led to the custom of children hanging stockings or putting out shoes, eagerly awaiting gifts from Saint Nicholas. Sometimes the story is told with gold balls instead of bags of gold. That is why three gold balls, sometimes represented as oranges, are one of the symbols for St. Nicholas. And so St. Nicholas is a gift-giver.

One of the oldest stories showing St. Nicholas as a protector of children takes place long after his death. The townspeople of Myra were celebrating the good saint on the eve of his feast day when a band of Arab pirates from Crete came into the district. They stole treasures from the Church of Saint Nicholas to take away as booty. As they were leaving town, they snatched a young boy, Basilios, to make into a slave. The emir, or ruler, selected Basilios to be his personal cupbearer, as not knowing the language, Basilios would not understand what the king said to those around him. So, for the next year Basilios waited on the king, bringing his wine in a beautiful golden cup. For Basilios' parents, devastated at the loss of their only child, the year passed slowly, filled with grief. As the next St. Nicholas' feast day approached, Basilios' mother would not join in the festivity, as it was now a day of tragedy. However, she was persuaded to have a simple observance at home—with quiet prayers for Basilios' safekeeping. Meanwhile, as Basilios was fulfilling his tasks serving the emir, he was suddenly whisked up and away. St. Nicholas appeared to the terrified boy, blessed him, and set him down at his home back in Myra. Imagine the joy and wonderment when Basilios amazingly appeared before his parents, still holding the king's golden cup. This is the first story told of St. Nicholas protecting children—which became his primary role in the West.

One of the oldest stories showing St. Nicholas as a protector of children takes place long after another story tells of three theological students, traveling on their way to study in Athens. A wicked innkeeper robbed and murdered them, hiding their remains in a large pickling tub. It so happened that Bishop Nicholas, traveling along the same route, stopped at this very inn. In the night he dreamed of the crime, got up, and summoned the innkeeper. As Nicholas prayed earnestly to God the three boys were restored to life and wholeness.

In France the story is told of three small children, wandering in their play until lost, lured, and captured by an evil butcher. St. Nicholas appears and appeals to God to return them to life and to their families. And so St. Nicholas is the patron and protector of children.

But despite the never ending versions of Santa in the mainstream arena I again see an inner story of genetics and brain functions dealing with the ancient code of human consciousness and here's how: The Holy Claustrum (Santa Claus) coordinates the input and output across the brain and creates what is known consciousness, a familiar theme by now.

So this is how the story really goes!

The Claustrum (Santa Claus) is located (lives) in the human head as part of the Cortex, which is at the very top of the body, our internal North Pole! The Claustrum is surrounded by White Matter (snow) in the brain. Directly next to it can be found the External and the Extreme Capsule which resemble a sleigh. It is also lateral to the Putamen ("consideration" - Latin putare: "to consider, to think" – awareness/consciousness), which is symbolized by the red cap that is worn by Santa Claus. The Putamen is connected to the Substantia Nigra (Latin: "black substance"), which is the symbolic coal of the chimney. This part of the brain is involved in the process of regulating reward (the promise of a gift or gifts in the case of the Santa story) and addictions and appears dark because it contains high levels of Neuromelanin. A unique feature of the Claustrum is that there is uniformity in the function of its cells, all Neurons do the same work and these Neurons are Santa's Elves, his famous and magical helpers. The suture of the skull (Suture = the process of joining two surfaces or edges together) is the external entry point (chimney) of the planetary Santa Claus, where he enters your head (roof top). The internal chimney is the human spine, the highway between the different levels of consciousness and facilitator between the two polar consciousness opposites.

Santa's reindeers are symbolic of a journey and the journey in this case, as with all other chapters in this book, is the journey between our inner consciousness and our outer consciousness as we strive towards our own personal transition. And there of course eight of them which then takes us back to the 'Ground Consciousness' of the Egypt section.

So there you have it, the story of Santa is really the inner workings of the brain and body.

So merry Christmas and enjoy the festivities, I still do.

Your reward this year is secret knowledge.

ו

Pirates:
The Inner Treasure

If like me you grew up as a teenager in the 1980's with movies such as the Goonies, Treasure Island and others or even if you are from a more modern era with the likes of Pirates of the Caribbean you will be aware of the thieves of the high seas, the Pirates. The likes of 'Treasure Island' is an adventure novel by Scottish author Robert Louis Stevenson, narrating a tale of "buccaneers and buried gold". Its influence is enormous on popular perceptions of pirates, including such elements as treasure maps marked with an "X", schooners, the Black Spot, tropical islands, and one-legged seamen bearing parrots on their shoulders. The search for treasure marked on the famous treasure map the finder of which would be guaranteed the accumulation of riches. The parrot on their shoulder, the eye patch covering one eye and the wooden ship showing the flag of death, the skull and crossbones. The famous pieces of 8 takes us back to the 'Ground Consciousness' mentioned in the Egyptian chapter.

The skull and cross bones are a symbol of death, or at least this is the most understood meaning of this symbol but what if that death was the death of the 'Old Testament' that marked the birth of a 'New Testament'? And by testament I refer to its actual meaning of body and mind! So what if this whole creation of the pirate and their symbols was actually telling us something deeper, so deep in fact that we cannot see it because it is referring to the most neglected aspect of life, which is ourselves? It is historically apparent that there were robbers and thieves on the high seas, but is there a deeper meaning hidden within the standard context? The skull and crossbones are also associated with secret societies and by virtue of this fact it has a hidden meaning.

I have over the last several years, but more concentrated over the past 12 months, delved deep into the world of the esoteric, particularly ancient cultures. I have found that they all portrayed a message and that message was one of self-enlightenment, reached by the magic of their monuments which show us how they did it. It was an advanced knowledge that has stood the test of time.

So with this in mind I can see a clear connection in the whole pirate philosophy and here's how:

For the religious people out there especially Christians, their Christ was crucified in Golgotha, the place of skulls and there is the first clue. The skull, or head, is where the Christ consciousness exists. I have explained that the Christ, or more to the point the Christ seed, is crucified on the cross which is the Optic Chiasm (known as the crossing) inside the brain, where 'X' marks the spot and of course 'X' also marks the spot on a Treasure map. So there we have the skull and crossbones, the symbol of Osiris in Egypt and the pathway to Christ consciousness within the mind which is the hidden meaning of this symbol.

The covering of one eye with an eye patch, is symbolic of either the eye of Horus or Isis (Right eye is Horus, Left eye is Isis) and the eye patch holds relevance to this. Isis and Horus make up two component parts of the three master gland system of the third eye.

Spiritually, in animal symbology, the Parrot represents the immense power of our inner mind, which again is connected to consciousness, thought being the prerequisite to manifestation and conscious connection to the higher realms.

So what about the hidden treasure?

Treasure in these stories is most prominently Gold and Gold is connected to enlightenment and also the Sun which aids our enlightenment, but we need to find it, we need to dig and retrieve what is within and find the treasure, or in other words, the collection of wisdom held within our skull and its third eye system. The pieces of eight refer to the Eight-Circuit Model of Consciousness that suggests eight periods and twenty-four stages of neurological evolution. The eight circuits or eight brains operate within the human nervous system, each corresponding to its own imprint and direct experience of reality. And when we read the Treasure Island story we hear about the 'Black Spot'. The Black Spot is a literary device invented by Robert Louis Stevenson for his novel Treasure Island. In the book, pirates are presented with a black spot. When we again go back to ancient Egypt they had a Black Dot called the 'Aten' which is their representation of the Bindi in Hinduism and it marks the exact place of the Pineal gland, a part of our inner consciousness, the third eye.

So there is my take on the whole scenario of pirates, they are of course real, but when we look into the world of symbology a different language is often being spoken.

With this symbology now decoded the treasure has been found.

18

Above Government: Crop Secret

So this whole book has spoken about the hidden language of consciousness. But what if our own planet Earth had such consciousness awareness and abilities? In terms of the sacred geometric patterns on the landscape that may well be the case.

The pattern on the landscapes is all over the world but predominantly located in sacred Wiltshire in the UK and it has baffled many and stirred the emotions of others. Is it Doug and Dave's wooden pole handy work or the work of something more advanced and complex? They have even been discovered within snow, without any footprints or regional disturbance like there would have been if people had walked there to create them. Crop circles were first documented over 200 years ago.

In the July of 2009 Sarah and I went to Wiltshire to visit some crop circles and with a twist of fate our tour guide told us that the BBC were with him that day filming a documentary about crop circles. The host was British actor Danny Dyer and we spent an interesting day filming with him and the camera crew. When I visited Wiltshire and stood inside a newly formed crop circle I could feel a warm energy field around me, it was a cold and rainy day yet inside the circle it was warm and pleasant. Many have eluded that these circles are an ET message for us to decipher, many have seen plasma balls of light creating them and others lay claim to creating them at night with planks of wood. I would only need to ask one question of those who make the claim that they used wood to create them, namely did you also use a computer? Obviously not, in which case explain how you created the Mandelbrot set crop circle in the 1990's which is so mathematically complex that it can only be reproduced by the precision of a computer!

I have made a personal journey from the paranormal and supernatural to the world of science and have combined the two to get my current state of mind and universal views. The majority of these circles are created near to the region of Stonehenge and this is for good reason, the land there is sacred and is a nexus of Earth's Leyline networks. This is why Stonehenge was built there. There is a universal supernatural force that we are still trying to discover, we know it exists but science is trying to prove it exists and fathom out how it works.

I am now going to take that blueprint and explain the crop circle phenomenon. Firstly in sacred geometry the circle is the divine shape which is relevant and the line is the sacred shape of partition which is also relevant. The Greeks called geometry 'Music Frozen' as it bears resemblance to musical notes and their mathematical nodes. An example of this can be found on YouTube with the Chladni plates. When we see a snowflake and its beautiful patterns we don't often realise that this is the shape of the sound of the environment around it and that the shape of that snowflake is purely a recreation of that sound's geometric patterns. The outside of the snowflake is an infinite fractal and the inside is a finite fractal in mathematical terms.

When people film and see plasma balls of light above an area which then sees a crop circle appear this is microwave energy and flash heat that causes one side of the crop to be elongated and therefore curved without damage, proving that even the greatest forces of nature can be gentle. This curvature gives us the crop circle formation using microwave energy which is a form of the universal energy electromagnetism. If electrons are floating around freely, even for a very short amount of time, they can be shoved far away from their point of origin by the electric field and then shoved back. And then forwards again. As they move back and forth, they crash into air molecules in the air that can knock electrons within them to higher-energy orbits. Then these electrons fall back, emitting light. That's why you have a glowing blob of plasma over a flame or in this case a flash heat. This plasma is hotter than the rest of the air and so it tends to rise up. This is how a microwave oven also works. And for those who are asking how microwave electromagnetic energy can form intricate shapes out of crops then this is for you.

Panpsychism is a branch of science that recognises that all things are conscious and therefore have a quality of awareness. When consciousness meets matter, matter is altered and at this epicentre of leyline activity crop circles are being formed by consciousness altering matter and its shape in a beautiful instantaneous amplification of force at ground level. Just like the artist conceives the idea and then manifests it onto canvass the universal energy that is yet to be understood is using sacred land as a canvass for its thoughts.

19

The Path Of Transcendence

It is not a matter for me to tell people how to live their lives or tell them what to do in their lives. But for those who wish to advance themselves and reach a higher plane of existence within this existence I am going to make a few suggestions. I have spoken about and written extensively about the wrongs in society and how we are all to some level and degree imprisoned and enslaved but many people are now asking for some solutions to help with escaping this regime.

"If you can't find the truth right where you are, where else do you expect to find it?" - Dogen Zenji

This is an excellent point because that's exactly where it is, within us, right where we are and all of the information I have shared in this book states just that, it is all within. It is just a matter of accessing it as it lies dormant within. The brain is a muscle too that needs exercising otherwise it becomes dormant and our mind (inner consciousness) cannot connect to the higher mind (outer/higher consciousness) when this is the case. The book has given you the tools used by the ancients to remove limitations and by doing the same we can become so much more, which in turn can benefit the Human race as a whole.

We have an identity, an essence which is what we truly are which is not Christian or Islam, Catholic or Hindu, Republican or Democrat, Labour or Conservative, or even black or white (which is merely electromagnetic frequency causing different skin pigmentation). We are much more at our deepest levels. Even the simplest of things such as not watching the mainstream news, or at least not believing the script at face value written by those who want to forge your reality. Choosing not to concentrate on negativity, as they do, which causes the neurons of the brain to form new pathways, a path of least resistance that attracts even more negativity because that becomes the new you, forming a negative path. It only leads to a victim mentality stopping people getting back to their true essence and true self. It is a trap that we need to look beyond and we also need to look at what is happening behind us whilst our attention is focused in front of us. We are the living spirit called 'human', encased within a material form, symbolised by the mummy case, we are a sleeping Christ.

We can help ourselves by eating organic food, rich with solar photons that connect to our genetic essences, drinking distilled water that has had the additives and shutting down of consciousness impurities removed. We can nourish knowledge which for me on a personal level has advanced me to levels that are above where I started in 2009 and by some considerable height. Knowledge is a powerful tool to have by your side and to know what the Gnostics know puts us all on a level playing field in which to act and rectify the mess we find ourselves in as a race of beings on planet Earth.

You can also listen to various frequencies to raise your vibrations and awareness and they have been highlighted throughout the book such as:

432 Hertz – The God frequency – that balances the third dimension

126 Hertz – Unity consciousness – transcendental frequency

528 Hertz – The love vibration and the miracle tone that restores human consciousness to its fullest power and potential

174 Hertz – Activates super consciousness

421 Hertz – which speeds up spiritual development

728 Hertz – Energy and cellular cleansing and balancing frequency

33 Hertz – Christ Consciousness

8 Hertz – Alpha brain waves and altered state of consciousness

31.32 Hertz – pure frequency for pituitary gland stimulation

936 Hertz – Pineal gland third eye awakening/inner light

Humans have been documented as carrying out superhuman activities, sometimes in situations of emergency and stress but sometimes through a pure enlightened vessel like many of the Asian and other cultures. If we could return to our full potential we would be capable of superhuman feats which are really our natural state of being. For example levitation where a person just floats in the air without any visible support.

For instance, the 16th-century mystic St Teresa of Avila was observed on many occasions, typically when deep in prayer, to rise anywhere from a few feet to as high as the ceiling of the room. When she felt an 'attack' coming on she would beg the sisters in her convent to hold her down, though they were not always successful. Once while receiving Holy Communion from the Bishop of Avila, she felt her knees begin to leave the floor so she clutched onto the grille. But after receiving the sacrament, she let go and rose into the air.

The 17th century Franciscan monk St Joseph of Copertino began levitating during services and was often observed by whole congregations. Once while walking in the monastery grounds, he soared up into the branches of an olive tree and remained kneeling on a branch for half an hour, the thin stem hardly moving under his weight. Unable to glide down, after his ecstasy had passed, he had to wait for a ladder to be brought. For 35 years he was banned from all public services, but he levitated not only before the Pope and his fellow monks but also before Europe's titled heads and the philosopher Leibnitz. The Spanish ambassador to the papal court watched him fly over the heads of a crowd to a statue of the Virgin Mary, where he briefly hovered. After giving his customary shriek, he flew back, the ambassador's wife had to be revived with smelling salts. The duke of Brunswick hid himself in a stairway to observe one of Joseph's levitations. After observing a second levitation, the duke renounced his Lutheran faith and became a Catholic. At Osimo, Joseph flew eight feet into the air to kiss a statue of Jesus then carried it off to his cell and floated about with it. He is also reported to have caught up another friar and carried him in the air around the room.

The annals of 19th-century spiritualism contain many references to human levitations, as well as to tables, chairs, and other objects gaining or losing weight, levitating, and moving without human contact.

The most famous levitator of all was the medium Daniel Dunglas Home (pronounced: Hume). His first recorded levitation took place at a seance in August 1852. He was suddenly 'taken up into the air, he palpitated from head to foot with the contending emotions of joy and fear. Again and again he was taken from the floor, and the third time he was carried to the ceiling of the apartment, with which his hands and feet came into gentle contact.' He later became able to levitate at will, and believed he was lifted up by 'spirits'. During a public career spanning 30 years, hundreds of people witnessed his levitations. The most famous incident was when in the company of Lord Adare, the Master of Lindsay, and a friend of theirs, he floated out of one window of a London house and in at another. The eminent English scientist Sir William Crookes saw him levitate on several occasions and verified that there was no trickery involved. On one occasion, Crookes' wife, who was sitting beside Home, was raised off the ground in her chair.

The magician Harry Kellar, who enjoyed showing audiences how mediums did their tricks, described how during a world tour in the 1870s he was watching a Zulu witch doctor go into a trance when suddenly 'to my intense amazement, the recumbent body slowly arose from the ground and floated upward in the air to the height of about three feet, where for a while it floated, moving up and down'. In 1882 he challenged the medium William Eglinton to perform some feat which no conjuror could repeat. Eglinton then levitated, carrying Kellar, holding his foot, into the air – an achievement which Kellar had to admit he could not explain.

The Italian medium Eusapia Palladino occasionally used to levitate and was also able to increase or decrease the weight of objects. Her paranormal powers were verified in investigations conducted by European scientists around the turn of the 20th century. After witnessing her demonstrations, the French astronomer Camille Flammarion stated that levitation should no longer be any more in question than the attraction of iron by a magnet. In the 1920s Brazilian medium Carlos Mirabelli performed stunning phenomena under test conditions. Full-form materializations of deceased individuals known to the witnesses appeared who were able to converse with the investigators, and to touch and be touched. He was also able to levitate and remain floating for minutes at a time. In one instance, a chair with Mirabelli in it rose into the air until it was two metres above the floor, where it remained for two minutes. Levitations of mediums have frequently been reported since then in spiritualist journals.

We know from Quantum tunnelling that we can walk through walls and this phenomenon is well documented and even understood under the bizarre rules that govern the microscopic world called quantum mechanics. Now, scientists have measured the timing of this passing-through-walls trick more accurately than ever before, where sub-atomic particles can travel back and forth in time. This occurs when a particle passes through a barrier that it seemingly shouldn't be able to. In this case, scientists measured electrons escaping from atoms without having the necessary energy to do so. In the normal world around us, this would be like a child jumping into the air, and somehow clearing a whole house. Quantum tunnelling is possible because of the wave-nature of matter. Confounding as it sounds, in the quantum world, particles often act likes waves of water rather than billiard balls. This means that an electron doesn't exist in a single place at a single time and with a single energy, but rather as a wave of probabilities.

For those of you who like I grew up as a teenager in the 1980's you would have seen classic films such as *Back to the Future!* A time travelling professor who travelled in time to other places. Recently in America a man claimed to be from 2048 who had come back to warn us of an alien invasion, he was drunk, but humanity must have survived that invasion if his claims are true, which is evident by his own survival! I don't happen to believe him though! But is time travel a credible possibility? According to Quantum Physics and more specifically Quantum Tunnelling, it is!

There was once a famous scientific experiment called the 'Double Slit' experiment where a Photon was shone through a single hole but it duplicated and made several lights upon the wall. The photons had split and duplicated themselves. It was noted that the photons behaved differently whilst under observation meaning that the photons had an awareness of being watched, a consciousness. It was also striking that this atomic structure was able to go back in time to change its behaviour, or what we would classify as time. It was also able to go forwards in time to the future and borrow energy which it brought back to this time in order to give itself an energy boost to enable itself to penetrate such things as solid objects, for example a wall, that it previously did not have the energy to do! We are made up of the same atomic elements and contrary to popular belief, we are not solid, we give off the appearance of a solid but we are molecules vibrating at a dense speed... This being the case then Time Travel is possible and highly credible. But have there ever been any cases of humans actually doing this? If particles can do this and we are made of particles then surely we can!

It is thought by many that there are monks in china that once practiced walking through walls. There was an incident where it was found that a human body was stuck in the middle of a concrete wall. This was explained by the monk practicing his walking through walls and then lost his concentration while he was inside and was unable to continue walking. The monk's molecules were intermixed with the molecules of the wall. But this could only happen if the electromagnetic force between the electrons in the person's atoms (person pushing) is greater than the force of the electrons in the wall's atoms.

Australian Aboriginal elders, Native American shamans, African sangomas, and many healers in native cultures throughout the world practice astral traveling. Numerous esoteric religions and philosophies are based on this experience. If a traditional healer was not able to physically travel to someone who was in need of healing, he would "travel by clouds". The pipe carrier would travel in a ceremonial way and enter via the sacred spirit tree in the centre of the home. They could not get into the home if they didn't enter through the tree. (Every home is said to have an invisible, yet very real spirit tree at its centre).

I have seen people out of body and I know it is real therefore we are more than just a physical body we are a much deeper essence within a physical body.

These are just a few examples there are also many other accounts of mystics levitating. It is a natural phenomenon that we have forgotten, as is the case with telepathy and telekinesis. All of our natural abilities shut down and de-programmed from our memory or consciousness. There have been instances where people have lifted cars in an emergency to release a trapped loved one from underneath it with superhuman strength. We are all potential superhuman and if some people can do this then we all can, it's a common human trait just waiting to be reconnected to our whole self.

We are not the lab rats and as previously mentioned the working ants of the colony running around for a Queen, we are more than this, in fact so much more and it's time we realised it!

20

Conclusion

Conclusion

So all the most famous biblical characters are living within us all and the wondrous ancient monuments are also replicating and representing the unseen universe within us too. Isn't that a good indication of our true potential and isn't that enough for those with sinister motives to want to keep that information away from us all? How unifying would it be in this world without the petty arguments over religions and gods, what if we could all unite behind one creator and just admit to ourselves and to each other that we are all a part of the same race and that there is no need or no place for division or segregation.

There is a hidden code that if discovered could change the game we play, we are merely pawns in another's game being moved across the chessboard of duality. This ancient and secret code gives you the key to enlightenment and knowledge and the establishment do not want you to know about it and it is therefore covered very cleverly behind stories so that it will not be found. It has fragmented to such an extent that piecing it back together is extremely difficult and seeing the whole picture itself is dependent upon having all of the pieces.

It was always a passion of mine to know the truth, even from a very young age I was very much different in that respect. I observed rather than spoke, I listened rather than comment and I pondered and contemplated rather than assume belief. I questioned why, and I questioned everything from a quiet and secluded corner of every room. Why do people believe what they believe, where does it come from and who is behind it? When I visited buildings of mystique I knew that within its Architecture was the answers, it contained a hidden language that only certain initiates could see, I soon began to read their script and I soon began to decipher their ancient language.

The esoteric truth hidden within, the key to enlightenment and success was pictorially concealed in glass and mortar. Celebrations of religious festivals meant something different to me than it did to the congregation and even the priests. I was the fish on land, the loner and the thinking man. The world seemed backwards to me, nothing followed a logical order, schooling taught me false history, society tried to teach me to accept slavery and governments tried to tell me that is was a good system.

There is a group of Aristocracy, for want of a better word, on this planet, that have kept secrets and knowledge away from the rest of us for thousands of years, never wanting us to know what they know.

This is known as the 'Philosophy of self-aggrandisement' personally using knowledge and information, for example, to secure yourself a better position in society or in power. And when you understand this you can see why we are kept in the modern day dark ages of false and contrived information. This arrives courtesy of our educational system, our news outlets, our so-called leaders and it forms our fake reality of an irrelevant celebrity culture that constantly rents out a place in our minds and occupies everything we read. We are living entirely within a fake low vibrational bubble that needs to be burst. They understand that if people were to ever realise their true potential then reliance upon an outside source would be unnecessary and that nullifies any need for Governments and banks and any other system of control and rule. When we buy something and we think it is our property, it isn't, we register it and Regis means king, we are handing it over to the state.

We are attacked by water, by air and by food, the gateway to our bodies to keep us just where we are needed to be. We have been duped into outside beliefs, such as false icons of rescue in the form of religious figures et al. We do not need them and when we know this then we have a good gage of our own personal development stage, all we ever need is within us and that is the secret that has been kept from us!

We are our own Salvation, WE! Ourselves!

This Knowledge is our rightful inheritance...

The world is under the grip of secret and hidden codes, a language that not many speak ciphered into the fabric of society, in its buildings, literature and its belief systems.

Break the codes and you speak the language!

But the one thing they are trying to prevent within us all is spiritual awareness.

Conclusion

The definition of spiritual is relating to or affecting the human spirit or soul as opposed to material or physical things. Many people state that they are spiritual and many of our ancient cultures all over the world practiced being conscious and they showed us that fact in their fantastic mysterious monuments, which I have deciphered. From the Egyptians all the way around the globe! But there is a scientific explanation for what 'Spiritual Awareness' is and it also takes us back to ancient Egypt in many ways, but I will detail one aspect of this connection…

The human brain holds many mysteries that we don't yet understand. Consciousness is simply a 'Quality of Awareness' or being aware of being aware' and enlightened or enlightenment means to transcend normal consciousness (beyond normal awareness). This is a scientific explanation for what is called a 'Neuropsychological Awakening', so as more awareness reaches us the more we reach that enlightened consciousness. So with every person that becomes aware of the information we strive to pass on to them they are getting closer to this height!

It is a harsh truth that the human race and human body is under constant attack and it is all by design to stop people ever deciphering these ancient ground-breaking codes of enlightenment. What if I was to say that everything that you learn, everything you thought was true, everything you see on TV and everything that you read in your newspapers was part of a deliberate cover-up of truth? What if I was to say that a group of individuals at the helm of the planet have a grand plan called 'Social Engineering' to manipulate the global populations view and experience of reality, would you believe me? And what if I was to say that communism and alike was merely a smoke screen to harness the working classes into a globalisation plan by Zionist bankers, but was controlled from the same strings, therefore making Russia and America allies not enemies behind the curtain?

"World events do not occur by accident. They are made to happen, whether it is to do with national issues or commerce, most of them are staged and managed by those who hold the purse string" – Statement made by Denis Healey, former British secretary of Defence.

The whole world is under the control of a group of Zionist bankers and Satanist Kabbalists who are known as the 'Illuminati' and they are descendants of the famous Knights Templars. The famous Oscar statue is also a Knights Templar, Oscar meaning sac-or, sack of Gold and the red carpet is symbolic of their genetic Bloodline families. We are ruled by a Frankism agenda stemming from illuminati financed Jacob Franks. All illuminati are Freemasons but not all Freemasons are illuminati. The masonic lodges are nurseries and those who are corruptible or blackmailable will be allowed to rise into and know about the true plan, the rest will remain within their lodges at the lower levels believing that they have reached the highest!

If you wish to control what people know or the information that they have access to you simply buy up the news agencies. In London, for example, the press operate from Fleet Street and fleet means under the same control/ownership. The world is being steered towards a 'Novus ordo seclorum' a New World Order of Globalism with its world capital in Jerusalem, the Holy Lands of the Knights Templar conquests and liaisons with Kabbalist groups, the Cabals. The human mind, according to George Friedrich Wilhelm Hegel a 19th century German philosopher, cannot understand unless things are split into polar opposites such as black and white, left and right and so on, this is known as the 'Hegelian Dialect. Therefore when we see such things as the Republican and Democratic party in America or a Labour and Conservative party in England people, without knowing, are really referring to a thesis based on this Hegelian dialect and debate is more tuned to differences between the two parties rather than the issues that neither side is discussing, again a smoke screen of diversion.

Another form of Hegelian Dialect is a phrase called *Problem, reaction, solution.*

It was created in the 19th Century by Hegel to forward a particular agenda and steer a certain global course such as the current fight on terrorism.

When we see and hear of occurrences often on a global scale, but also commonly on a regional scale, just think and consider what is going on in the background behind the scenes and where it is really taking us. The plan is a secret plan but it's obvious when you can see it and can see through it with enough pieces of the jigsaw. Your religions, your society, your beliefs, your reality and your life, is manipulated by these minority groups who divide you with false teachings to keep you away from the truth.

To understand the moves you must first understand the game!

They use codes to hide the truth and a code is a method of communication but much more intriguing is hidden code, because hidden code is deliberate concealment. We live in a world full of hidden codes and secret languages that are only spoken by and understood by the initiates of the brotherhoods and not the average man/women on the street who simply pass them by each and every day. And this is completely deliberate! When you speak the coded languages of these initiates, when you know what they know, the world of their language becomes your own native tongue! I have deciphered their codes, I speak their language and I can tell you that our history is deliberately falsified. The world is not what you think it is and your reality is a contrived cover-up and none of this is by chance, it is all manufactured to be this way. I want to give people back their power. I am in deplorable mood when I see people starving in a world of plenty. I am not against capitalism but I see a problem when we pay soccer players millions every month and yet people die of hunger, people die waiting for hospital treatments and die of homelessness. I am also deplored when I see men and women working until they are too old to do anything after they retire and then to see their pensions stolen by tycoons or governments. When I see people chained by debt, which I know, is a fake system of control. And I am in deplorable mood when I see the people being continuously deceived and taken advantage of by a corrupt system and I want it to change for the benefit of all.

It is now time to start anew, we have the knowledge and we have the means. So in ancient philosophy let us resurrect and ascend to our rightful levels.

So there you have it, the ancient code is one of consciousness achieved through kundalini awakening (A Serpent Fire). And this is written within their magnificent monuments and literal works.

Thank you for your time in reading this book and I hope that the ancient and secret information helps you to levitate beyond this prison planet!

If we can all activate our third eye system and elevate ourselves to higher consciousness, then we will see the effects of this biblical scripture. Isaiah 11:6-9 *"The wolf will live with the lamb, the leopard will lie down with the goat, the calf and the lion and the yearling together and a little child will lead them. The cow will feed with the bear, their young will lie down together and the lion will eat straw like the ox. The infant will play near the cobra's den and the young child will put it's hand into the viper's nest. They will neither harm nor destroy on all my holy mountain for the earth will be filled with the knowledge of the lord as the water's cover the sea".*

Best wishes
Michael Feeley

michael@michael-feeley.com
www.michael-feeley.com

OTHER TITLES BY MICHAEL FEELEY

PAPERBACKS

Walk Into The Light – The Journey Of A Lightworker Duo
ISBN, 978-0-9566103-0-0
Beyond The Illusion – A Time Of Awakening
ISBN, 978-0-9566103-1-7
Earth Is An Experiment, Duality Is A Game... And Love Is The Answer
ISBN, 978-0-9566103-2-4
The Secret of Christ
ISBN, 978-0-9954554-5-0
The Secrets of The Pyramids
ISBN, **978-0-9954554-4-3**

EBOOKS

7 Things The Police Don't Want You To Know
ISBN, 978-0-9954554-6-7
Police Encounters of the Third Kind
ISBN, 978-0-9954554-7-4
When Murder Travels Through Time
ISBN, 978-0-9954554-8-1
Stonehenge - The Secret Of The Monoliths
ISBN, 978-1-912400-02-7

Available to purchase from

www.michael-feeley.com

Michael Presents His Talk, 'The Ancient Code'

If you would like Michael to speak at your venue please get in touch via his website: www.michael-feeley.com

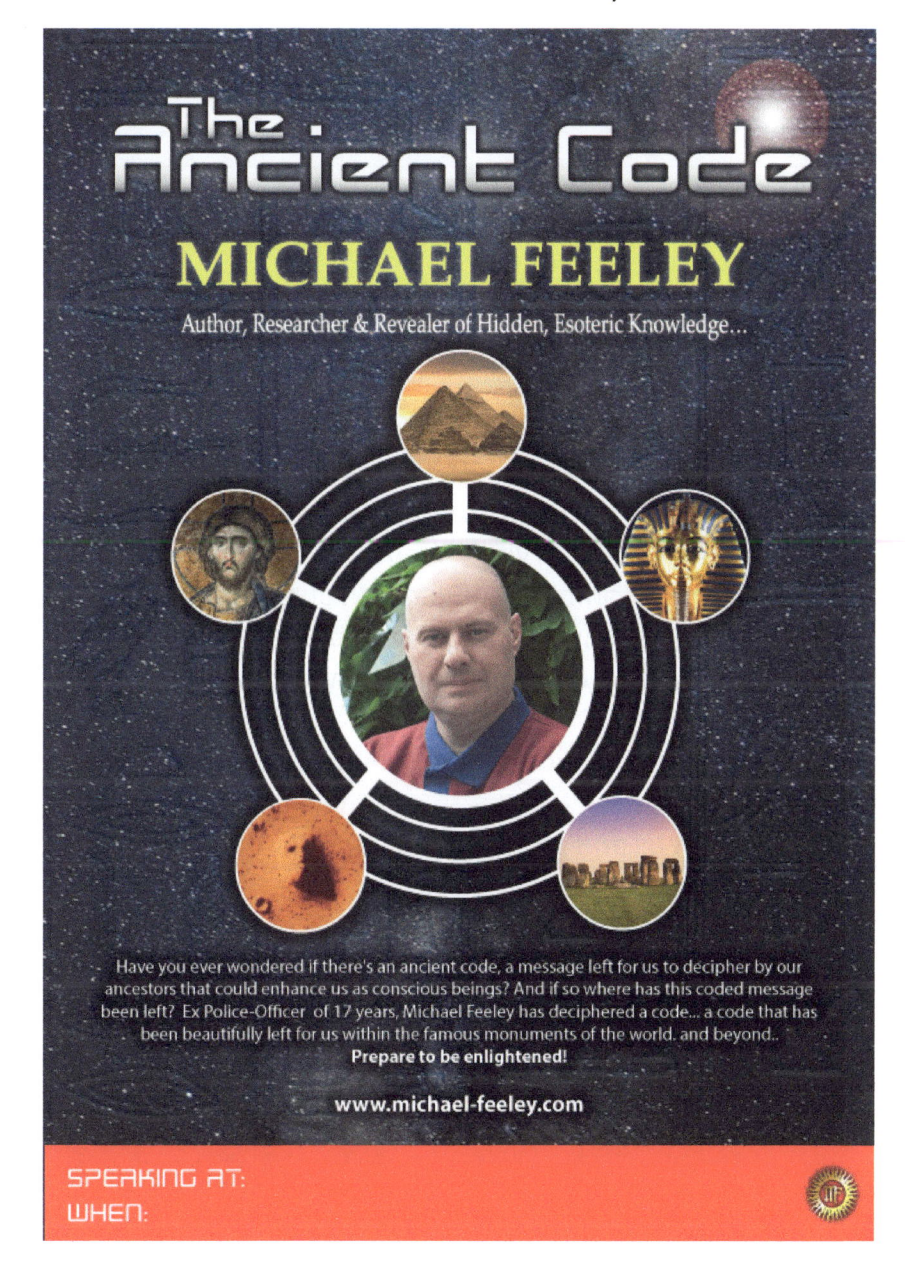

The Ancient Code
MICHAEL FEELEY
Author, Researcher & Revealer of Hidden, Esoteric Knowledge...

Have you ever wondered if there's an ancient code, a message left for us to decipher by our ancestors that could enhance us as conscious beings? And if so where has this coded message been left? Ex Police-Officer of 17 years, Michael Feeley has deciphered a code... a code that has been beautifully left for us within the famous monuments of the world, and beyond..
Prepare to be enlightened!

www.michael-feeley.com

SPEAKING AT:
WHEN:

Self-Publishing Your Book Made Easy!

Michael's Publisher Sazmick Books, offer self-publishing, editing and marketing services to authors of most genres. We help to fulfill your ambition of getting your work from typed or written manuscript, into a printed book or E-book with customisable add-ons.

Simple packages, Stunning books.

Chat with us and get your book on the road today!

www.sazmickbooks.com

For All Your Self-Publishing Needs